UNDERSTANDING
DEMOCRACY

A HIP POCKET GUIDE

JOHN J. PATRICK

Published in association with JusticeLearning.org

A Project of the Annenberg
Foundation Trust at Sunnylands

OXFORD
UNIVERSITY PRESS

OXFORD
UNIVERSITY PRESS

Oxford University Press, Inc., publishes works that further
Oxford University's objective of excellence
in research, scholarship, and education.

Oxford New York
Auckland Cape Town Dar es Salaam Hong Kong Karachi
Kuala Lumpur Madrid Melbourne Mexico City Nairobi
New Delhi Shanghai Taipei Toronto

With offices in

Argentina Austria Brazil Chile Czech Republic France Greece
Guatemala Hungary Italy Japan Poland Portugal Singapore
South Korea Switzerland Thailand Turkey Ukraine Vietnam

Copyright © 2006 by Oxford University Press, Inc.

Published by Oxford University Press, Inc.
198 Madison Avenue, New York, New York, 10016
www.oup.com

Library of Congress Cataloging-in-Publication Data
Patrick, John J.-
Understanding democracy / John J. Patrick.
p. cm.
"Published in association with JusticeLearning.org."
ISBN-13: 978-0-19-531197-6
ISBN-10: 0-19-531197-3
1. Democracy–United States. 2. United States–Politics and
government.
I. JusticeLearning.org. II. Title.
JK1726.P36 2006
320.473—dc22
2006007416

Printing number: 9 8 7 6 5 4 3 2 1

Printed in the United States of America
on acid-free paper

Contents

An Introduction to Democracy 5
Accountability 16
Authority 17
Citizen 18
Citizenship 19
Civic Education 20
Civil Society 22
Common Good 24
Constitution 26
Constitutionalism 28
Democracy, Representative and Constitutional 31
Diversity 33
Elections 36
Equality 37
Federalism 39
Government, Constitutional and Limited 42
Independent Media 44
Judicial Independence 45
Judicial Review 46
Justice 49
Liberalism 52
Liberty 56
Majority Rule and Minority Rights 58
Market Economy 60
Parliamentary System 62
Participation 65
Pluralism 68
Political Party 70
Popular Sovereignty 73
Presidential System 76
Republic 79
Republicanism 82
Rights 84
Rule of Law 88
Separation of Powers 90
Social Democracy 94
State 96
Unitary State 97
Virtue, Civic 98
Further Reading 100
Websites 101
Index 104

AN INTRODUCTION TO DEMOCRACY

We live in an era of democracy. A majority of the world's people live in countries with a democratic form of government, and many others desire democracy. This is a startling new development.

During most of the 20th century, there was mortal conflict between democracy and its rivals, and the nondemocratic side often seemed to be winning the struggle. In 1920, for example, there were only 15 democracies in the world, and at mid-century fewer than one-third of the world's people lived in the 22 established democratic countries. By the end of the 20th century, however, democracy was ascendant; nearly two-thirds of the world's people lived in the more than one hundred countries with a democratic form of government. The global advancement of democracy has continued into the 21st century.

What exactly is democracy? When and where did it begin? What are the differences between democracy in ancient and modern times? How do we know the difference between democracy and non-democracy today? What is the universal problem of good government in a democracy? What are arguments for and against democracy? And why do citizens of a democracy need to know exactly what it is and is not?

The Origin of Democracy in Ancient Times

Although democracy is newly resurgent, it is an old idea. More than 2,500 years ago in Athens and other cities of Greece (*Hellas*), there was rule (*kratia*) by the people (*demos*). Democracy (*demokratia*), or rule by the people, was an alternative to such traditional governments as monarchy, rule by one, and oligarchy, rule by the few.

In the first democracies, citizens made and enforced the laws for their small republic, the *polis* or community of the city. There was majority rule by the *citizens,* the people of the *polis* who participated directly in their assembly, the lawmaking body. The status of citizen, however, was restricted to free males of Greek descent, a minority of the population. Women and slaves could not be citizens, and only a small number of non-Greek males ever were granted the privilege of citizenship.

Ancient Greek democracy afforded citizens equal rights to participate directly in governance for the common good of their community. The claims of the community upon the person, however, were primary and superior to the claims of the person upon the community. A good citizen was expected to serve unconditionally the interests of the city-community, especially to defend its freedom and independence against the threat of foreign domination.

There was no sense of personal and private rights of individuals in the democracies of ancient Greece. The decisions made by a majority vote of citizens often disregarded the interests of those in the minority, and sometimes the citizen majority formed a tyranny that abused and oppressed individuals with unpopular opinions.

The Differences between Democracy in Ancient and Modern Times

Democracy today is very different from its ancestors in antiquity. As in the past, democracy today is government of, by, and for the people, but modern democracy involves government by the people acting indirectly through their elected representatives, rather than government conducted directly by the people themselves, as in antiquity. And the large-scale nation-state—very different in size and complexity from the small Greek *polis*—is the typical domain of the modern democratic government.

In striking contrast to the limited definition of citizenship in ancient times, democracy today is inclusive; nearly all permanent inhabitants of a country may possess or acquire the rights and privileges of the citizen and thereby claim membership among the people of the polity. Most important, modern democracy works by majority rule in tandem with protection of minority rights. Tyranny of the majority over minorities is considered unjust in a democracy of our time—a gross flaw to be avoided, and if it occurs something to be corrected immediately.

The idea of liberty in today's democracies differs significantly from that in ancient times. Democracy in our world implies both collective and personal liberty. There is concern for civic unity and the public good, as in ancient times, but diversity and privacy matter, too. Differences in opinions and interests are tolerated and even encouraged in the public and private lives of citizens. Unlike democracy in ancient times, which directed citizens primarily to serve the community, the primary purpose of government in a modern democracy is to serve and protect all persons under its authority and especially to secure their inherent rights to liberty and safety.

How to Distinguish Democracy from Non-Democracy Today

There is broad international agreement today about the minimal criteria a country must meet in order to cross the threshold of democracy. In an authentic democracy, the citizens or people choose representatives in government by means of free, fair, contested, and regularly scheduled elections in which practically all adults have the right to vote and otherwise participate in the electoral process. Between elections, all persons living in a genuine democracy can participate freely to influence the decisions of their government. And members of minority parties are able to criticize and otherwise oppose the ruling party or parties without obstruction in their pursuit of victory in the next electoral contest to control the government. Popular sovereignty prevails; the government rules by consent of the people to whom it is accountable.

An authentic democracy of our time is anchored in a constitution, a framework for limited government that guarantees the rule of law to protect the political rights of individuals to freedom of speech, press, petition, assembly, and association. Thus, citizens can participate freely to elect their representatives in government and to hold them accountable during the period between elections. And they can freely associate and express their individuality and diversity in civil society, the private domain of life that exists independently of control by government. A legitimate constitution functions effectively in the daily lives of individuals to prevent the government from acting arbitrarily to impose either a tyranny of an elite group over the majority or a tyranny of the majority over unpopular minorities.

The primary characteristics of democracy today, which distinguish it from non-democracy, are constitutionalism, representation in government, and individuals' rights to liberty. Constitutionalism provides limited government and the rule of law based in a constitution. Representation of the people in government comes by way of free, fair, competitive, and periodic elections conducted in accordance with a constitution that protects individuals' rights to participate. And the ultimate desirable consequence of constitutionalism and representative government through elections is the guarantee of rights to liberty for each person in the nation, majorities and minorities alike. Thus, liberty in an indirect or representative democracy depends upon constitutionalism, which limits and regulates the power of government in order to guard against tyranny of any kind.

Constitutionalism in a democracy especially protects against the pitfall of majority tyranny, which has afflicted popular governments of times past and present. Only by constitutionally restraining the majority to protect the rights of minorities can there be inclusion of all the people in the polity, a necessary condition for justice in a democracy today.

The Universal Problem of Good Government in a Democracy

Constitutionalism involves tension between power in government required to maintain order among the people and limits on power to prevent government from unjustly denying liberty to the people. This inescapable tension raises a fundamental and universal problem for any people who aspire to achieve or maintain constitutional democracy. How can a society combine liberty and order for the purpose of securing equally and justly the rights of all persons in the nation?

This universal problem was discussed in an acclaimed collection of papers written to encourage ratification of the

U.S. Constitution, *The Federalist*, co-authored in 1787–88 by three founders of the United States of America: Alexander Hamilton, James Madison, and John Jay. In the 51st paper of *The Federalist*, Madison defined the problem of liberty and order in constitutional government:

> But what is government itself but the greatest of all reflections on human nature? If men were angels, no government would be necessary. If angels were to govern men, neither external nor internal controls on government would be necessary. In framing a government which is to be administered by men over men, the great difficulty lies in this: you must first enable the government to control the governed, and in the next place oblige it to control itself. A dependence on the people is, no doubt, the primary control on the government; but experience has taught mankind the necessity of auxiliary precautions [a well-constructed constitution].

Madison recognized that the individual's rights to political and personal liberty are at risk if the government has too much power or too little power. If the government's power is too strong, or insufficiently limited, then it can and probably will be used to oppress certain individuals and deprive them unjustly of their right to liberty. There must be constitutional limits upon the power of government in order to protect the rights of all members of the community.

However, if the government is too limited, or insufficiently empowered, it will be incapable of maintaining law and order and protecting individuals against domestic or foreign predators, who could deprive them of their rights to life, liberty, and property. So, a good government in a democracy is both sufficiently limited and empowered by a constitution, to which the people have consented, for the achievement of order that secures liberty.

It is a daunting challenge for the people of a democracy to create, establish, and maintain such a constitutional government. Observance of constitutional limitations is the key to meeting this challenge. A good constitution limits the power of the people's representatives in government to prevent them from abusing individuals' rights to liberty, and it empowers the government to limit licentious expressions of liberty in order to prevent rampant disorder that could destroy democracy. Thus, when the government threatens the rights of individuals it is constrained, and when individuals threaten the authority of government they are checked. The result is ordered liberty, the solution to the universal problem of how to achieve good government in a representative and constitutional democracy.

The direct democracies of ancient times did not adequately balance liberty and order. This failure led to critical deficiencies that doomed them, such as disruptive factional conflict, excessive demands by the city-community on the citizens, tendencies toward majority tyranny, disregard of personal or private rights, and inept or unjust enforcement of law and order. In 1787, James Madison wrote in his 10th paper of *The Federalist*, "such democracies have ever been spectacles of turbulence and contention; have ever been found incompatible with personal security or the rights of property; and have in general been as short in their lives as they have been violent in their deaths."

The papers of *The Federalist* include remedies to the deficiencies of past democracies. These proposed remedies influenced the development and improvement of representative democracy in the United States of America and in other modern democratic republics. The principal and overarching remedy to the ills of direct democracy was this: to establish and maintain a representative government, a democratic republic, empowered and limited by the supreme law of a well-constructed constitution to protect equally the liberty and other fundamental rights of all persons in the polity.

Every sustainable democracy responds more or less adequately to the universal problem of how to combine liberty and order in one constitutional government. But, although some people have done better than others, there has never been a perfect response to this problem. A genuine democracy today is constitutional and representative. Protecting equal rights to liberty of all persons in a democracy, however, depends primarily upon constitutionalism, the indispensable guarantor of representative government and individual rights.

Arguments For and Against Democracy

Ever since ancient times, democracy has had its proponents and detractors. For most of human history, the critics of democracy have far outnumbered its advocates. Only within the last two hundred years has support for democracy in its constitutional and representative form gained momentum. And only within the past 50 years have the promoters of democracy in the world greatly outnumbered its opponents. Among the major claims of its proponents are the propensities of democracy to:

- enhance the individual's sense of dignity and self-worth
- encourage individuals to promote the well-being of their community
- provide equal opportunities for individuals' self-fulfillment
- draw upon the collective wisdom of the people in making decisions
- treat individuals as political and civic equals
- protect the equal rights of all persons to life, liberty, and property
- encourage economic productivity and a high quality of life by distributing rewards based on merit rather than inherited status
- promote international peace, order, and stability, because democracies tend not to fight against each other
- bring about orderly resolution of conflict within a country
- make rulers accountable to the people they rule
- justify the legitimacy of government by basing it on popular consent

Opponents of democracy dispute the claims of its advocates. Some major deficiencies of democracy, say the detractors, are its tendencies to:

- govern inefficiently due to excessive deliberation in decision making
- govern ineptly because the most able persons are not selected to rule
- make unwise decisions in government by pandering to public opinion
- erode political and social authority and unity by encouraging criticism and dissent
- obstruct excellence by catering to conventional ideas and to the lowest common standards among the masses of the people
- overemphasize political and social equality to the detriment of liberty
- encourage abuse or disregard of unpopular persons and opinions
- discourage innovation and creativity by ignoring or marginalizing unpopular sources of ideas and artistic expression
- fail to achieve its ideals or to adhere to its basic principles

Most people in the world today believe the strengths of democracy greatly exceed its weaknesses. The case for democracy has been greatly augmented by the demise in the 20th century of prominent non-democracies, such as the Japanese Empire, Nazi Germany, Fascist Italy, the Union of Soviet Socialist Republics, and communist dictatorships in central and eastern Europe. The acceptance of democracy by countries of diverse histories and cultures—such as Argentina, Germany, India, Italy, Japan, Mexico, the Philippines, Poland, Portugal, South Africa, and Sweden—indicates a pervasive desire for freedom and self-government throughout the world.

It seems that, given a choice, people throughout the world will opt for democracy and the liberty it secures as the surest political means to fulfilling their needs and aspirations. The great 20th-century British political leader Winston Churchill recognized that democracy, despite its shortcomings, was better than the alternatives, declaring, "Democracy is the worst form of government, except all those other forms that have been tried from time to time."

Despite its widespread popularity, it is clear that democracy is not and cannot be a utopia. Its wisest proponents neither promise nor pursue absolute political and social perfection through democracy. Rather, they recognize the inevitable disparities in every democracy between ideals and realities, and they expect that citizens in every democracy will fail occasionally to fulfill its highest ideals and defining principles.

Its apparent imperfections do not invalidate the ideals and principles of democracy. Throughout the history of democracy in the United States and elsewhere, the standards by which democracy is defined have inspired citizens to persevere in a never-ending quest to narrow the gap between lofty ideals and flawed realities and to practice its principles more exactly and authentically. Although the highest standards of democracy remain unrealized, they nonetheless have been catalysts for improvements in the political and civic lives of people throughout the world.

Why Citizens Need to Know the Core Concepts of Democracy

The establishment and maintenance of a democracy depends greatly upon effectively educating the people about the differences between constitutional democracy and various other types of government. If there would be "government of the people, by the people, for the people"—Abraham Lincoln's pithy phrase about the meaning of democracy—then there must be education of the people about what it is, how to do it, and why it is good, or at least better than the alternatives to it. Confounded concepts of democracy inevitably lead to confused and flawed practices of it, putting at risk the future of this form of government.

During the past century, rulers of nondemocratic regimes appropriated the vocabulary of democracy to mask their dictatorial control of the people. Despotic regimes, such as the fallen Soviet Union, the defunct Democratic Republic of (East) Germany, the Democratic Republic of (North) Korea, and the People's Republic of China, used showcase constitutions that proclaimed governments of the people and the defense of human rights to confound their opponents and justify their existence. In such corrupt regimes, there were constitutions without constitutional governments and guarantees of human rights without the practical protection of them. These wrongful uses of the vocabulary and trappings of democracy demonstrated dramatically the importance of teaching citizens the concepts by which genuine democracy can be distinguished from its bogus imitators and rivals.

The great 19th-century French philosopher Alexis de Tocqueville feared that flawed definitions of democracy would confuse people's understanding of it and threaten its very existence. So, he bequeathed a wise warning about definitions and uses of words to the defenders of democracy against despotism. He said,

> It is our way of using the words "democracy" and "democratic government" that brings abut the greatest confusion. Unless these words are clearly defined and their definition agreed upon, people will live in an inextricable confusion of ideas, much to the advantage of demagogues and despots.

Tocqueville wanted people of the future to realize that if they were unable to tell the difference between an authentic democracy and its counterfeit imitators then government of, by, and for the people would be at risk, an unfortunate circumstance that afflicted many countries during most of the 20th century. The sage advice of Tocqueville guided the planning and writing of this little book. Its reason for being is improving public understanding of the words by which democracy is understood and practiced throughout our world today. If more and more people are able to identify an authentic democracy, then democracy in our time might be more faithfully practiced and its blessings more extensively enjoyed. Toward this end, the core concepts of democracy are presented alphabetically in the subsequent pages.

These concepts are, collectively, the criteria by which we can know what democracy is and what it is not. They are generic categories that enable us to analyze and appraise how democracy is practiced in countries throughout the world. These core concepts may be practiced differently among the various countries of our world, but every genuine democracy is based upon them in one way or another. And, if they are missing or slighted in a country claiming to be a democracy, then its claims are false.

The vocabulary of democracy in this little book denotes knowledge that should be possessed in common by citizens of the United States of America and any other democracy in order to make this form of government work better for them. If they would be supporters and promoters of democracy against its detractors and critics, then citizens of a democracy need to know its essential characteristics.

Accountability

Accountability means that the government in a democracy is responsible to the people for its actions. This responsibility is primarily ensured by periodic public elections through which the people choose their representatives in government. If those elected to represent the people are insufficiently responsive to them, they are likely to be rejected at the next election and replaced by others who promise greater accountability.

Both elected and appointed officials in government are held accountable to the people by laws that regulate their actions. These laws limit the government's use of power in order to protect the people from abuse. There also are laws that require transparency or openness in government so that the people may readily have information necessary to evaluate the performance of their elected and appointed officials.

The mass media of communication, such as newspapers, television, radio, and websites, provide the public with information about the performance of government. Laws that protect freedom of speech and of the press are therefore foundations of accountability in a democracy. In particular, the mass media regularly conduct public opinion polls to measure the people's approval or disapproval of particular representatives or of the government in general. Thus, independent and privately owned media outlets provide the people and their representatives with information that prompts accountability by the government to the governed.

Some democratic governments, such as those in Sweden, Lithuania, and Estonia, include the office of *ombudsman*, an appointed official who responds directly to individuals with a grievance against the government and who is empowered to seek resolutions of complaints. Most democracies also include agencies that regularly conduct evaluations of the performances of different parts of the government and communicate their findings to the public.

SEE ALSO Civil Society; Elections; Independent Media; Popular Sovereignty

Authority

Authority is the legitimate use of power by rulers over the individuals they rule. It is a government's justification for exercising power over the people within its jurisdiction. The people are willing to accept the power of rulers to command them, if they perceive that this power has been acquired and used rightfully or legitimately. When rulers have authority to use power through government, the consequence is political order and stability among the people. When rulers use power without authority, they may be resisted by the ruled, leading either to oppression by rulers over the ruled or to disorder and instability.

In a democracy, the source of authority or *legitimacy* for government is the consent of the people, who believe that their rulers have the right to exercise certain powers over them. This legitimacy of government in a democracy is based on the people's election of representatives in the government. If the people believe their rulers have been elected fairly, then they are likely to accept their authority and consent to the government that they control. All the power of military and police forces in a democracy is under the control of civilian authorities accountable to the people at large.

Authority in a democracy, which is based on consent of the people, is distinct from authoritarianism. An authoritarian government exercises power on other grounds of legitimacy. For example, authoritarian justifications for legitimacy to rule have been aristocratic birth or the sanction of a Supreme Being (which is commonly known as the divine right to rule). In an authoritarian government, the military and police are commanded by rulers who are not directly accountable to the people they rule.

SEE ALSO Elections; Popular Sovereignty

Citizen

A citizen is a full and equal member of a political community, such as a country or nation-state. Such membership is a necessary condition for the establishment and maintenance of a democracy. The citizens are "the people" to whom a democratic government is accountable.

In most countries, the status of a natural citizen is derived primarily or even exclusively from one's parents; if the parents are citizens, then their children automatically become citizens, too. If one does not have a birthright to citizenship, either through one's parents or place or birth, there usually are legal procedures by which a person can become a *naturalized* citizen of a country. A country's constitution and the laws based on it specify the means for obtaining the status of citizen. For example, the 14th Amendment of the U.S. Constitution says, "All persons born or naturalized in the United States, and subject to the jurisdiction thereof, are citizens of the United States and of the State wherein they reside."

In a democracy, all citizens, both natural and naturalized, are equal before the law. For example, the constitution of Italy says, "All citizens have the same social dignity and are equal before the law, without discrimination of sex, race, language, religion, political opinion, and personal or social conditions." In a constitutional democracy, all citizens have the same fundamental rights, duties, and responsibilities.

All citizens have a common *civic identity* based on their freely given consent to basic principles and values of their country's constitutional democracy. In countries with great religious, racial, or ethnic diversity, a common civic identity among all citizens is the tie that binds them together under their constitutional and democratic government.

A passport is evidence of a person's status as a citizen of a particular nation. A citizen of one country usually needs a passport to enter and depart legally from another country.

SEE ALSO Citizenship; Government, Constitutional and Limited; Popular Sovereignty; State

Citizenship

Citizenship is the legal relationship between citizens and their government and country. Citizens owe their government loyalty, support, and service. The government owes the citizens the protection of constitutionally guaranteed rights to life, liberty, property, and equal justice under law.

The rights of citizenship are set forth in the constitution of a democratic government, which may distinguish between the rights of citizens and noncitizens within the country. For example, in the United States, only citizens have the right to vote, serve on juries, and be elected to certain offices of the government, and only a natural-born citizen can become President. All other constitutional rights are guaranteed to citizens and noncitizens alike.

Citizenship in a democracy entails serious responsibilities. For example, good citizens in a democracy exhibit *civic engagement,* which means they are ready, willing, and able to use their constitutionally protected political rights to advance the common good. Citizens are expected to be loyal and patriotic, to assume responsibility for the defense of their country against internal and external threats or attacks. Citizenship also entails certain duties, such as paying taxes, serving on juries when summoned, joining the country's armed forces if drafted, and obeying the laws.

In the world today, citizenship is the fundamental condition that connects individuals to the protective institutions of a democratic government and provides the means through which they can participate politically and civically in their governance. The rights, responsibilities, and duties of citizenship in a democracy have practical meaning today only within a particular kind of political order, a constitutional democracy. Only within the authority of a democratically governed country are there dependable institutional means to enforce constitutional guarantees of rights.

SEE ALSO Citizen; Civil Society; Government, Constitutional and Limited; State

Civic Education

A democracy depends upon the competent participation of its citizens in government and civil society. This can only happen when the people are educated for citizenship in a democracy. Therefore, all democratic countries provide formal and informal opportunities for civic education, or teaching and learning about citizenship. Formal civic education is carried out through the curriculum of schools, and informal civic education occurs through the interaction of individuals in various societal organizations.

Civic education is teaching the knowledge, skills, and virtues needed for competent citizenship in a democracy. Unlike despotic forms of government, in which the people are merely passive receivers of orders from their rulers, democracy involves a significant measure of independent thinking and popular decision making. A democracy cannot be maintained unless the citizens are educated sufficiently to carry out certain duties and responsibilities of a self-governing people, such as voting intelligently, communicating effectively about public issues, cooperating with others to solve common problems, and making judgments about the performance of their government.

Wherever in the world democracy exists, schools are expected to prepare students for citizenship through civic education. The society outside the school also provides lifelong opportunities for civic education through the mass media and by participation in community service organizations and political parties.

The primary component of civic education is imparting the knowledge needed for citizens' informed participation in their democracy. Informed citizens have basic knowledge of such subjects as history, economics, geography, and government or political science. They comprehend core concepts of democracy, the constitution and institutions of democracy in their own country, and public issues in the past and present pertaining to the practice of democracy.

A second component of civic education is developing the intellectual and practical skills that enable citizens to use knowledge effectively as they act individually and collectively in the public life of their democracy. These skills include the capacities of citizens to read, write, and speak effectively; to think critically; and to make and defend sound judgments about public issues. Skills of thinking and participating, in combination with civic knowledge, enable citizens with common interests to influence the decisions of their representatives in government.

A third component of civic education is encouraging the virtues that dispose citizens positively to the ideals and principles of their democracy. Examples of these civic virtues are civility, honesty, charity, compassion, courage, loyalty, patriotism, and self-restraint. These character traits prompt citizens to contribute to the well-being of their community and democracy.

Civic education is needed to maintain democracy, because citizens fit for self-government are made, not born. The preservation of democracy in any country requires that each generation of the people learn what their democracy is, how to participate responsibly and effectively in it, and why they should try to keep and improve it.

SEE ALSO Citizen; Civil Society; Participation; Virtue, Civic

Civil Society

Civil society is the network of voluntary associations, or nongovernmental organizations, that are separate from the institutions of the government but subject to the rule of law. Apart from the government, civil society is a private domain that serves the public good. Some examples of the nongovernmental organizations that comprise civil society are independent labor unions, churches and other formal religious organizations, professional and business associations, private schools, community service clubs, and the privately owned media (independent newspapers, radio stations, television stations, websites). Persons in a constitutional democracy are free to belong simultaneously to many nongovernmental organizations. Thus, they may freely associate with like-minded persons to promote mutual interests.

A vibrant civil society is an indicator of good civic behavior in a constitutional democracy. It shows that many citizens are willing to donate their time, energy, and money in order to improve their community. It also demonstrates that citizens are using their constitutional rights to freedom of association, assembly, speech, and press. Through their civic participation in nongovernmental organizations, individuals develop the knowledge, skills, and virtues of citizenship in a democracy. Thus, the voluntary associations of civil society are community laboratories in which citizens learn democracy by doing it.

In stark contrast to a genuine democracy, a totalitarian government, which attempts to concentrate all power in a centralized state dominated by one political party, does not permit a free and open civil society to exist. In the now-defunct Soviet Union, for example, the only civic groups were those formed and maintained by the dictatorial government. There were labor unions, but they were neither independent nor free of government control. There were mass media, but the government owned and managed them in order to prevent people from transmitting information contrary to the interests of the rulers.

The maintenance of a lively civil society depends upon constitutionalism. The constitutional government in a democracy is the guarantor of the individual's rights to freedom of speech, press, assembly, and association, which are necessary to the formation and independent actions of civil society organizations. And the rule of law emanating from the constitution is the basis for public safety and order, which in turn enable civil society organizations to function and thrive. Civil society organizations, however, are not only protected by constitutionalism, but they are also protectors of it. Dynamic networks of free and independent nongovernmental organizations, including free and independent media, have resources that enable them to resist despotic tendencies of the government.

Alexis de Tocqueville wrote in his classic work *Democracy in America* about the tension that exists between free civil associations and government:

> An association for political, commercial or manufacturing purposes, or even for those of science and literature, is a powerful and enlightened member of the community . . . which, by defending its own rights against the encroachments of government, saves the common liberties of the country.

Civil society is an opponent of despotic tendencies in government and an ally of genuine constitutional democracy. Free and private civil associations often act in harmony with governmental institutions but they also tend to check an abusive or liberty-threatening exercise of state power. Thus, the nongovernmental organizations that constitute civil society can collectively be a countervailing force against a government that tries to nullify the constitutional liberties of its people.

SEE ALSO Common Good; Constitutionalism; Government, Constitutional and Limited; Independent Media; Participation; Pluralism; State

Common Good

The common good (sometimes called the *public good*) may refer to the collective welfare of the community. It also may refer to the individual welfare of each person in the community.

A *communitarian* view of the common good in a democracy is equated with the collective or general welfare of the people as a whole. The well-being of the entire community is considered to be greater than the sum of its parts, and the exemplary citizen is willing to sacrifice personal interests or resources for the good of the entire community. The good of the country or the community is always placed above the personal or private interests of particular groups or individuals. From this communitarian perspective, the ultimate expression of the common good is the elevation of public or community interests above private or individual interests.

When viewed individualistically, however, the common good is based on the well-being of each person in the community. In a democracy, the government is expected to establish conditions of liberty and order that enable each person to seek fulfillment and happiness on his or her own terms. The exemplary citizen respects and defends the individual rights of each person in the expectation of reciprocity from others. From the perspective of *individualism,* the ultimate achievement of the common good is when the rights of each person in the community are protected and enjoyed equally.

In most democracies of our world today, both the communitarian and individualistic conceptions of the common good are expressed and somehow combined. In particular countries, however, there usually is a tendency to favor one idea of the common good more than the other. In the United States, for example, the individual interest model of the common or public good tends to prevail. By contrast, in Japan and Poland for example, the collective sense of public good is dominant. In these democracies, the general good of the community, and the people as a whole, is usually considered to be more important than the interests or needs of any individual within that community.

In every democracy of our world, there is some degree of tension—in some countries higher and in others lower—between the perceived rights and interests of individuals and the communitarian idea of a common good. In the second volume of *Democracy in America*, published in 1840, the French political philosopher Alexis de Tocqueville wrote about the necessity for citizens to blend personal and public interests in order to achieve and maintain the common good.

Tocqueville referred to this kind of citizenship as "self-interest rightly understood" because, through some reasonable voluntary contributions of time, effort, and money to the civil society and government, citizens cooperated to maintain the conditions of public safety, order, and stability needed to successfully pursue their personal interests and liberty. They recognized that their personal fulfillment could not be attained unless the general welfare of their community was strong. Tocqueville wrote, "The principle of self-interest rightly understood is not a lofty one, but it is clear and sure. . . . Each American knows when to sacrifice some of his private interests to save the rest."

SEE ALSO Citizenship; Civil Society; Liberalism; Republicanism; Virtue, Civic

Constitution

A constitution is the basic law and general plan of government for a people within a country. The purposes, powers, and limitations of government are prescribed in the constitution. It thus sets forth the way a people is governed or ruled.

A constitution is the supreme law of a country. Laws later enacted by the government must conform to the provisions of the constitution. All institutions, groups, and individuals within the community are expected to obey the supreme law of the constitution.

A constitution is a framework for organizing and conducting the government of a country, but it is not a blueprint for the day-to-day operations of the government. The Constitution of the United States of America, for example, is less than 7,500 words long. It does not specify the details of how to run the government. The officials who carry out the business of the constitutional government supply the details, but these specifics must fit the general framework set forth in the U.S. Constitution.

A defining attribute of a democratic constitution is its granting and limiting of powers to the government in order to guarantee national safety and unity as well as individuals' right to liberty. It sets forth generally what the constitutional government is and is not permitted to do. There cannot be an authentic democracy unless the powers of government are limited constitutionally to protect the people against tyranny of any kind.

Constitutions vary in length, design, and complexity, but all of them have at least seven common attributes: (1) a statement of the purposes of government, usually in a preamble; (2) specification of the structure of government; (3) enumeration, distribution, and limitation of powers among the legislative, executive, and judicial functions of government; (4) provisions about citizenship; (5) guarantees of human rights; (6) means of electing and appointing government officials; and (7) procedures for amendment.

Most countries of the world today have a constitution that is written in a single document. A very few countries, such as Israel, New Zealand, and the United Kingdom, have "unwritten" constitutions. These so-called unwritten constitutions are composed of various fundamental legislative acts, court decisions, and customs, which have never been collected or summarized in a single document. However, as long as an unwritten constitution really limits and guides the actions of the government to provide the rule of law, then the conditions of constitutional government are fulfilled.

The Constitution of the United States, written in 1787 and ratified by the required nine states in 1788, is the oldest written constitution in use among the countries of the world today. However, the constitution of the state of Massachusetts was written and ratified in 1780 and, although extensively amended, is still operational, which makes it the world's oldest written constitution in use today. Most of the world's working constitutions have existed only since 1960, and many of the world's democracies have adopted their constitutions since 1990.

SEE ALSO Constitutionalism; Democracy, Representative and Constitutional; Government, Constitutional and Limited

Constitutionalism

Constitutionalism is a way of thinking about the relationship between the rulers and the ruled in a community. It combines two concepts, *limited government* and the *rule of law*, that permeate the constitution, a country's framework for government. The constitution in an authentic democracy both grants powers to the government and controls or harnesses them in order to protect the rights of the people.

Limited government means that officials cannot act arbitrarily when they make and enforce laws and enact other public decisions. Government officials cannot simply do as they please. Rather, they are guided and limited by the constitution of their country and the laws made in conformity with it as they carry out the duties of their public offices.

The *rule of law* means that neither government officials nor common citizens are allowed to violate the supreme law of the land, the constitution, or the laws enacted in accordance with it. People accused of crimes are treated equally under the law and given due process—that is, fair and proper legal proceedings—in all official actions against them. Under the rule of law, everyone in the community—public officials and private citizens, from the highest to the lowest ranks—must conform to the constitution.

In every democracy today, limited government and the rule of law are embedded in the constitution. For example, the 1976 constitution of Portugal says:

1. Sovereignty, one and indivisible, rests with the people, who shall exercise it in accordance with the forms laid down in the constitution.
2. The state shall be subject to the constitution and based on democratic legality.
3. The validity of the laws and other acts of the state, the autonomous regions or local authorities shall depend on their being in accordance with the constitution.

A turning point in the history of constitutionalism occurred in 1787–88, when the U.S. Constitution was drafted and ratified. The Preamble stated the purposes of the constitutional government:

> We the people of the United States, in Order
> to form a more perfect Union, establish
> Justice, insure domestic Tranquility, provide
> for the common defence, promote the general
> Welfare, and secure the Blessings of Liberty
> to ourselves and our Posterity, do ordain and
> establish this Constitution for the United
> States of America.

In order to carry out its purposes in the Preamble, the government under this constitution was sufficiently empowered to protect the people. And the constitutional government was sufficiently limited so that the government would not be able to turn its power unjustly against the people. Thus, this simultaneously strong and limited government would "secure the Blessings of Liberty" to the people.

Article 6 of the Constitution states the principle of constitutional supremacy that guarantees limited government and the rule of law: "The Constitution and the Laws of the United States which shall be made in Pursuance thereof . . . shall be the supreme Law of the Land." All laws enacted by any government in the United States must conform to the Constitution. As Alexander Hamilton explained in the 78th paper of *The Federalist*, "No legislative act contrary to the Constitution, therefore, can be valid." Moreover, any government action that violates the Constitution can be declared unconstitutional and voided by the U.S. Supreme Court.

In 1787–88, Alexander Hamilton and James Madison claimed in *The Federalist* that limited government and the rule of law—principles essential to the U.S. Constitution—would guard the people from tyranny or unjust encroachments against their right to liberty. They feared equally any kind of unrestrained exercise of power. To them, the power of an insufficiently limited majority of the people was just as dangerous as the unlimited power of a king or military dictator.

Hamilton and Madison held that the best government is both constitutionally empowered and limited; it is "energetic"—strong enough to act decisively and effectively for the common good—and "limited by law" in order to protect the inherent rights of individuals. These principles of constitutionalism expressed by Americans in the late 18th century have become guides to the establishment of constitutional governments in many democracies of the world.

SEE ALSO Constitution; Democracy, Representative and Constitutional; Government, Constitutional and Limited

Democracy, Representative and Constitutional

Democracy in the governments of countries today is *representative*, meaning that the people rule indirectly through their elected public officials. Democracy today is also *constitutional*, meaning that government by the people's representatives is both limited and empowered to protect equally and justly the rights of everyone in the country.

Representatives elected by the people try to serve the interest of their *constituents* within the framework of a constitutionally limited government. The constitution ensures both majority rule and minority rights.

The U.S. government is a prime example of representative and constitutional democracy. It is a representative democracy because the people, the source of its authority, elect individuals to represent their interests in its institutions. The formation and function of the government is based on majority rule. The people, for example, elect their representatives by majority vote in free, fair, competitive, and periodic elections in which practically all adult citizens of the country have the right to vote. Further, the people's representatives in Congress make laws by majority rule. A chief executive, the President, elected by the people, then enforces these laws.

Representative democracy in the United States is constitutional because it is both limited and empowered by the supreme law, the Constitution, for the ultimate purpose of protecting equally the rights of all the people. The periodic election by the people of their representatives in government is conducted according to the Constitution and the laws made under it. The votes of the majority decide the winners of the election, but the rights of the minority are constitutionally protected so that they can freely criticize the majority of the moment and attempt to replace their representatives in the next election. From time to time, there is a lawful and orderly transition of power from one group of leaders to another. Legitimate legal limitations on the people's government make the United States a constitutional democracy, not an unlimited democracy in which the tyranny of the majority against political minorities could persist without effective challenges.

In earlier autocratic governments, the unrestrained power of a king or an aristocracy had typically threatened liberty. However, Alexander Hamilton, James Madison, and other framers of the U.S. Constitution feared that a tyrannical majority of the people could pose a new challenge to liberty. Madison expressed his fear of majority tyranny in an October 17, 1788, letter to Thomas Jefferson:

> Wherever the real power in a Government lies, there is the danger of oppression. In our Governments, the real power lies in the majority of the Community, and the invasion of private rights is chiefly to be apprehended, not from acts of Government contrary to the sense of its constituents, but from acts in which the Government is the mere instrument of the major number of the constituents. This is a truth of great importance, but not yet sufficiently attended to.... Whenever there is an interest and power to do wrong, wrong will generally be done, and not less readily by [a majority of the people] than by a ... prince.

Madison foresaw that in a representative democracy a threat to individual's liberty could come from an unrestrained majority. Unless they are effectively limited by a well-constructed constitution, which the people observe faithfully, the winners of a democratic election could persecute the losers and prevent them from competing for control of the government in a future election. This kind of danger to liberty and justice can be overcome by constructing and enforcing constitutional limits on majority rule in order to protect minority rights.

SEE ALSO Constitution; Constitutionalism; Elections; Government, Constitutional and Limited; Rights; State

Diversity

In a constitutional democracy, there is bound to be diversity among the people. It may be expressed as diversity in ideas and interests, diversity in social and political groups, diversity in religion, race, and ethnicity, and diversity in centers of power.

Diversity in the expression of ideas and interests is a product of the guaranteed rights to free speech, press, and religion that typify a constitutional democracy. In a constitutional democracy, there is a free marketplace of ideas in which differences of opinion may compete for public acceptance. Oliver Wendell Holmes Jr., a great justice of the U.S. Supreme Court, recognized that constitutionally protected freedom to exchange ideas can point the way to truth and progress. He wrote in his dissenting opinion in *Abrams* v. *United States,* 1919, "The best test of truth is the power of the thought to get itself accepted in the competition of the market. . . . That at any rate is the theory of our Constitution."

In a free society, there will always be a diversity of competing interests voiced openly by different individuals and groups. Interests will vary, for example, according to occupation, social status, and gender. Owners of businesses are likely to express and campaign for different interests in comparison to members of trade unions or agricultural groups. Lower-income persons are likely to favor and actively seek some kinds of public assistance that would be of less interest to individuals in higher earning brackets, who are likely to pursue other kinds of benefits from the government. Women have some interests that differ from those of men, and they are free to advance these interests through public discussion and debate.

A constitutional democracy protects rights to freedom of expression, assembly, and association, which encourage diversity among groups. Like-minded individuals choose to form and join civic and political associations in order to promote their opinions and interests. There is a multiplicity of cooperating and competing nongovernmental organizations that comprise a free and open civil society.

Political parties are a prominent example of the freedom to associate and assemble, a freedom that prevails in every genuine constitutional democracy. The constitution protects the political right of people with similar ideas and interests to organize and participate in political parties, which compete to advance their ideas and interests about how to conduct the government.

Many democracies include a diversity of religious, ethnic, or racial groups. In India, for example, there are many different ethnic groups with different languages and customs. The Indian constitution protects the rights of these different groups to express openly and freely their diverse ways of life. The constitution of India recognizes the multicultural diversity of the country by reserving a certain number of seats in parliament for representatives of different ethnic groups.

Some democracies, such as Switzerland, are constituted to accommodate the special interests of constituent ethnic groups. The preamble to Switzerland's constitution asserts that the Swiss people will "live its diversity in unity." The constitution formally preserves the three major ethnic groups of Switzerland: French, Italian, and German. There is a constitutional guarantee of two kinds of identities. First, every citizen possesses in common a Swiss *civic identity*, regardless of differences in ethnicity. Second, citizens of Switzerland also possess a distinct ethnic identity connected with one of their country's constituent cultural groups.

Like India, Switzerland, and other democracies, there is freedom in the United States for diversity to flourish among different ethnic, racial, and religious groups. There are constitutional guarantees of rights to freedom of expression, assembly, and association, which protect everyone—including members of vulnerable minority groups—against certain kinds of unjust treatment. In order to protect the civil liberties and rights of black Americans, who had endured particular injustices, the 13th, 14th, and 15th Amendments were added to the U.S. Constitution following the Civil War. These amendments prohibit slavery or involuntary servitude, guarantee citizenship and basic legal procedural rights on equal terms to all individuals, and prohibit the federal or state governments from denying the right to vote due to "race, color, or previous condition of servitude." Despite these constitutional guarantees of equal treatment under the Constitution, black Americans continued to suffer various kinds of unfair treatment. Through the heroic efforts of the 20th-century civil rights movement, black Americans used their rights under the Constitution to achieve a greater measure of justice under the law. However, unlike the constitutional democracies of India and Switzerland, the U.S. Constitution does not require special representation of ethnic or racial groups in the government. And constitutional rights in the United States are guaranteed generally to individuals and not to particular social groups.

A most important kind of diversity in an authentic constitutional democracy is variation in centers of power. The primary center of authority and power, of course, is the government, but there are other centers of power that are vital to diversity in a democracy. For example, a diverse democracy includes a free and open civil society in which various nongovernmental groups collectively form a center of power that protects individuals' liberty from excessively centralized government power. Another constitutionally secured center of power in a democracy is the free and open market economy through which the diverse owners of private property and wealth can be a countervailing force against the danger of despotism.

Yet another type of diversity in centers of power is the constitutionally guaranteed autonomy or quasi-independence of local government units, which share power with the central government of the country. For example, in the Federal Republic of Germany there is a division of powers between the federal government in Berlin and the various *Lander* or constituent states of the federal system. Such a division of power among different levels and units of government is a means to limit power and protect liberty in a democracy.

SEE ALSO Federalism; Market Economy; Participation; Pluralism; Political Party

Elections

A primary defining characteristic of democracy is the regular occurrence of free, fair, competitive elections in which practically all the people of a country can vote to select their representatives in government. Elections are not authentically democratic if there is only one candidate for each office or if only one political party is permitted to present candidates. Nor can a genuine electoral democracy stop or discourage significant numbers of persons from becoming citizens or from voting by using such onerous methods as physical intimidation, difficult procedures, and unfair tests of knowledge. If the government or a single political party controls or dominates the mass media, there cannot be the free flow of reliable information required for fair competition between rival candidates and political parties, and the consequence is a less than fully democratic election.

In the United States, there is a two-party system. Candidates from the two major political parties, Democratic and Republican, are the dominant competitors for election to positions in government, and candidates of minor political parties have little or no chance to win an election. However, minority parties can influence the outcome of an election by attracting a significant number of voters away from one of the major parties. In most democracies, there is a multiple-party system in which candidates from several political parties have a chance to win an election.

Elections in a democracy usually contribute to the stability and legitimacy of government. Citizens who participate in the elections have a sense of connection to their government and an expectation that it will be responsive to them. In return, they are likely to obey laws readily, pay taxes promptly, and contribute voluntarily to the common good of their country.

SEE ALSO Accountability; Authority; Participation; Political Party

Equality

Equality in a constitutional democracy means equal justice under the law. No one is above or beyond the reach of the law, and no one is entitled to unfair advantages or subjected to unequal penalties based on the law. Three main examples of equality in a democracy are constitutionally guaranteed protection for equality of treatment according to the law, equality in fundamental human rights, and equality of citizenship.

Statements about equality of treatment under the law are found in the constitutions of every democratic state. For example, Article 29 of the Lithuanian constitution says,

> All people shall be equal before the law, the court, and other State institutions and officers. A person may not have his or her rights restricted in any way, or be granted any privileges, on the basis of his or her sex, race, nationality, language, origin, social status, religion, convictions, or opinions.

The 5th and 14th Amendments of the U.S. Constitution guarantee legal equality, too. The due process clauses of the 5th and 14th Amendments require that the federal and state governments must follow fair and equal legal procedures in matters pertaining to an individual's rights to life, liberty, and property. The 14th Amendment says, "No state shall . . . deny to any person within its jurisdiction the equal protection of the laws."

Equality in the possession of fundamental human rights is another essential attribute of every constitutional democracy. This idea of equality was dramatically put forward in the 1776 Declaration of Independence, which proclaimed to the international community the emergence of a newly independent country, the United States of America. The declaration asserted a self-evident truth: that each person is born with equal possession of certain inherent rights, such as the right to "Life, Liberty, and the Pursuit of Happiness." Further, this declaration held, "That to secure these Rights, Governments are instituted among Men."

The founders of the United States were not claiming that all individuals are equal in their personal attributes, such as physical strength, intelligence, or artistic talent. They were not saying that a government is established to enforce equality or uniformity in the way people think, act, or live. Rather, the founders were committed to establishing a government that would guarantee equally, to all individuals under its authority, security for liberty based on the rule of law. The idea of natural equality in rights, that every person inherently possesses fundamental rights stemming from his or her equal membership in the human species, has been expressed in the constitutions of democracies throughout the world.

Equality of citizenship is another characteristic of constitutional democracies today. There are not degrees of citizenship whereby, for example, some persons have first-class citizenship with superior rights and privileges relative to different classes of citizens with different rights. Thus, Article 4 of the U.S. Constitution says, "The Citizens of each State shall be entitled to all Privileges and Immunities of Citizens in the several States."

SEE ALSO Citizen; Citizenship; Democracy, Representative and Constitutional; Justice; Liberalism; Rights; Rule of Law

Federalism

Modern federalism is the division of governmental powers between a central national government and provincial or state governments within the country. Powers granted exclusively to the central government are supreme. Federalism differs from the unitary system of government, which has only one center of authority that prevails throughout the territory of the country. In a unitary system, subdivisions within the country are entirely subordinate to the national government and exist merely to administer or carry out its commands.

The idea of modern federalism was invented by the framers of the United States Constitution. It was their way to bring together 13 separate and sovereign American states into one federal union, the United States of America. It was also one constitutional means, among others, to limit the powers of government to prevent tyranny against the people.

In a modern-era federal republic, there are two levels of government—one national and general in scope and the other local. Each level of government, supreme in its own sphere, can separately exercise powers directly upon the people under its authority.

In traditional forms of federated government, known today as confederations, the states, provinces, or other units of government within the union retained full sovereignty over their internal affairs. The general governments of such confederations only had a few powers pertaining to the need for common foreign policies and defense against external enemies. The Articles of Confederation, by which the United States was formed initially, established a federation of the traditional type, nothing more than a league of sovereign states joined together primarily for purposes of common defense and international relations.

By contrast, the constitution of 1787, which superseded the Articles of Confederation, included a "supremacy clause" in Article 6. This clause declares that the constitutional powers delegated to the federal or general government take precedence over the powers of the state governments, and that these powers prevail throughout the nation, the United States of America.

In the American federal system, the national (federal) government has certain powers that the Constitution grants to it alone. For example, only the federal government may coin money or declare war. Conversely, the Constitution reserves to the state governments all the other powers that the federal government is not granted. According to the U.S. Constitution's 10th Amendment, "The powers not delegated to the United States by the Constitution, nor prohibited by it to the States, are reserved to the States respectively or to the people." Only the state governments may establish public schools and conduct elections within the state. Some powers, such as levying taxes and borrowing money, are shared by both federal and state governments, and some powers, such as granting titles of nobility, are denied to both the federal and state governments.

The core idea of American federalism is that two levels of government, national and state, exercise certain powers directly and separately on the people at the same time.

This is known as a system of dual sovereignty. So, in the federal system of the United States, the state government of Ohio has authority over its residents, but so does the federal government based in Washington, D.C. Residents of Ohio must obey the laws of their state government and their federal government.

In the 45th paper of *The Federalist,* James Madison gave his vision of how federalism would work in the United States of America:

> The powers delegated by the Constitution to the federal government are few and defined. Those which are to remain in state government are numerous and indefinite. The former will be exercised principally on external objects, as war, peace, negotiation, and foreign commerce.... The powers reserved to the several states will extend to all objects which, in the ordinary course of

affairs, concern the lives, liberties, and
properties of the people, and the internal
order, improvement, and prosperity of the
states.

The balance of power within the American federal system has changed continuously since Madison's time to favor the national government. Through constitutional amendments, Supreme Court decisions, federal statutes, and executive actions, the powers of the federal government have greatly expanded to overshadow those of the states.

In addition to the United States, some other democracies that have federal systems of government include Argentina, Australia, Belgium, Brazil, Canada, Germany, India, Mexico, and Switzerland. In some nations, such as Belgium, India, and Switzerland, a federal system was adopted to reconcile tensions between national unity and the separatist tendencies of diverse ethnic groups with different languages and traditions. For example, the Swiss Federation was designed primarily to protect and preserve the ethnic and linguistic diversity of the three constituent ethnic groups—French, German, and Italian—within the unity of one nation-state, Switzerland.

In contrast to the multicultural federations of Switzerland, India, and Belgium, the protection of separate ethnic groups' interests was not the reason for federalism in the United States. Rather, it was to forge national unity among 13 separate states that had common cultural characteristics including the primary language of English and legal and constitutional traditions derived from Great Britain. So, in the United States, the national motto *E Pluribus Unum* (From Many, One) reflects the use of federalism to resolve the potentially destructive tensions between the particular interests of several state governments and the general interests of a federal or national government.

SEE ALSO Citizenship; Diversity; Government, Constitutional and Limited; State; Unitary State

Government, Constitutional and Limited

Government is the institutional authority that rules a community of people. The primary purpose of government is to maintain order and stability so that people can live safely, productively, and happily. In a democracy, the source of a government's authority is the people, the collective body of citizens by and for whom the government is established. The ultimate goal of government in a democracy is to protect individual rights to liberty within conditions of order and stability.

Every government exercises three main functions: making laws, executing or implementing laws, and interpreting and applying laws. These functions correspond to the legislative, executive, and judicial institutions and agencies of any government.

In an authentic democracy the government is constitutional and limited. A constitution of the people, written by their representatives and approved directly or indirectly by them, restrains or harnesses the powers of government to make sure they are used only to secure the freedom and common good of the people. There are at least five means to limit the powers of government through a well-constructed constitution.

First, the constitution can limit the government by enumerating or listing its powers. The government may not assume powers that are not listed or granted to it.

Second, the legislative, executive, and judicial powers of government can be separated. Different individuals and agencies in the government have responsibility for different functions and are granted constitutional authority to check and balance the exercise of power by others in order to prevent any person or group from using its power abusively or despotically. An independent judiciary that can declare null and void an act of the government it deems contrary to the constitution is an especially important means to prevent illegal use of power by any government official. The legislature can use its powers of investigation and oversight to prevent excessive or corrupt actions by executive officials and agencies.

Third, power can be decentralized throughout the society by some kind of federal system that enables the sharing of powers by national and local units of government. Widespread distribution of power to various individuals, groups, and institutions throughout a country can also be accomplished by constitutional protections of individuals' rights to form and maintain the voluntary associations of civil society and the economic institutions of a free market economy.

Fourth, the people can limit the power of government by holding their representatives accountable to them through periodic elections, which are conducted freely, fairly, and competitively according to provisions of the constitution. The people can also use their constitutionally protected rights of free speech, press, assembly, and association to mobilize force against abusive or irresponsible exercise of power by their government.

Fifth, a broad range of human rights can be included in the constitution, which the government is prohibited from denying to the people. In addition to such political rights as voting and expressing opinions through the media, the constitution can guarantee personal rights to private property, freedom of conscience, and so forth.

The existence of a written constitution does not always signify the practice of constitutional and limited government. There were written constitutions in Fascist Italy, Nazi Germany, and the Soviet Union, but there was not constitutional government. Instead, there was arbitrary use of power as it suited the rulers, irrespective of the wishes of the people. Thus, only governments that usually, if not perfectly, function according to the terms of a constitution may be considered examples of constitutional and limited government.

SEE ALSO Civil Society; Constitution; Constitutionalism; Democracy, Representative and Constitutional; Rule of Law; Separation of Powers

Independent Media

In a constitutional democracy, the mass media—newspapers, magazines, radio and television stations, and websites—are for the most part privately owned, independent, and free of government control. They are among the nongovernmental organizations of civil society, and they are free to transmit information and ideas about government and public affairs to the people. Therefore, they can criticize government officials and offer alternative opinions about current events and issues. By contrast, nondemocratic governments restrict the mass media in order to communicate only information that is supportive of public officials. In communist regimes, such as the defunct Soviet Union, the government owned and operated all mass media in order to indoctrinate the people and maintain control over them.

One function of the mass media in a democracy is to inform people about current events and introduce them to a variety of opinions about public issues. They thus enable the people to participate intelligently and responsibly in civic and political affairs. A second function is to criticize the government and expose the performance of public officials to public scrutiny, making the government accountable to the people it represents. Mistakes by government officials are more likely to be corrected, and government is more likely to be a responsible servant of the people than in countries with state-controlled media.

The mass media in a constitutional democracy have the right to freedom of expression. The government cannot, for example, restrain in advance what a newspaper may print. However, citizens may as consumers choose to reject or ignore particular newspapers or other media sources. Thus, there is a free market place of ideas in which citizens and communicators interact to exchange opinions about how to improve their democracy.

SEE ALSO Accountability; Citizenship; Civil Society; Constitutionalism; Rights

Judicial Independence

The judicial component of government is independent in order to insulate its members from punitive or coercive actions by the legislative and executive departments of the government. If the judiciary is independent, then it can make fair decisions that uphold the rule of law, an essential element of any genuine constitutional democracy.

The U.S. Constitution, for example, protects judicial independence in two ways. First, Article 3 says that federal judges may hold their positions "during good Behavior." In effect, they have lifetime appointments as long as they satisfy the ethical and legal standards of their judicial office. Second, Article 3 says that the legislative and executive branches may not combine to punish judges by decreasing payments for their services. The constitutions of some democratic countries provide appointments to the judges for a specific period of time, but invariably they protect their independence of action during their terms of office.

Alexander Hamilton, a framer of the U.S. Constitution, offered justification for an independent judiciary in the 78th paper of *The Federalist*. He wrote, "The complete independence of the courts of justice is peculiarly essential in a limited Constitution." Hamilton claimed that only an independent judicial branch of government would be able to impartially check an excessive exercise of power by the other branches of government. Thus, the judiciary guards the rule of law in a constitutional democracy.

SEE ALSO Constitutionalism; Government, Constitutional and Limited; Judicial Review; Rule of Law; Separation of Powers

Judicial Review

Judicial review is the power of an independent judiciary, or courts of law, to determine whether the acts of other components of the government are in accordance with the constitution. Any action that conflicts with the constitution is declared unconstitutional and therefore nullified. Thus, the judicial department of government may check or limit the legislative and executive departments by preventing them from exceeding the limits set by the constitution.

The concept of judicial review was created during the founding of the United States and specifically included in the constitutional governments of some of the 13 original American states, such as Massachusetts, New Hampshire, and New York. Judicial review is not mentioned in the U.S. Constitution, but most constitutional experts claim that it is implied in Articles 3 and 6 of the document.

Article 3 says that the federal judiciary has power to make judgments in all cases pertaining to the Constitution, statutes, and treaties of the United States. Article 6 implies that the judicial power of the federal courts of law must be used to protect and defend the supreme authority of the Constitution against acts in government that violate or contradict it. Article 6 says,

> This Constitution, and the Laws of the
> United Sates which shall be made in
> Pursuance thereof; and all Treaties made, or
> which shall be made under the authority of
> the United States, shall be the supreme Law
> of the Land; and the Judges in every State
> shall be bound thereby, any Thing in the
> Constitution or Laws of any State to the
> Contrary notwithstanding.

Furthermore, Article 6 states that all officials of the federal and state governments, including all "judicial Officers, both of the United States and of the several States; shall be bound by Oath or Affirmation to support this Constitution."

In 1788, in the 78th paper of *The Federalist*, Alexander Hamilton argued for judicial review by an independent judiciary as a necessary means to void all governmental actions contrary to the Constitution. He maintained that limits placed on the power of the federal legislative and executive branches in order to protect the rights of individuals "can be preserved in practice no other way than through . . . courts of justice, whose duty it must be to declare all acts contrary to . . . the Constitution void." Without this power of judicial review, Hamilton asserted, "all the reservations of particular rights or privileges would amount to nothing." Hamilton concluded,

> No legislative act, therefore, contrary to the Constitution can be valid. . . . [T]he interpretation of the laws is the proper and peculiar province of the courts. A constitution is . . . a fundamental law. It therefore belongs to [judges] to ascertain its meaning as well as the meaning of any particular act proceeding from the legislative body.

John Marshall, chief justice of the United States, applied the ideas about judicial review put forth in *The Federalist* in the 1803 case *Marbury* v. *Madison*. In this case, the U.S. Supreme Court declared one part of a federal law to be unconstitutional. In so doing, it set a precedent for the Court's use of judicial review, which became an essential part of constitutional democracy in the United States.

In the 20th century, judicial review was incorporated into constitutional democracies around the world. In most of them, however, the power to declare acts of government unconstitutional is called *constitutional review*—not judicial review—and it works a bit differently than it does in the United States. For example, the U.S. Supreme Court exercises judicial review, as do federal circuit courts of appeal and district courts, which also deal with various other cases that have nothing to do with constitutional issues.

In most other democracies, a special constitutional court, whose sole function is to consider the constitutionality of government actions, exercises constitutional review. Meanwhile, other courts resolve issues that pertain strictly to statutory interpretation, without any involvement of the constitutional court. The constitutional courts of other democracies may provide advisory or binding opinions about the constitutionality of an act separate from the adversarial process in which a real case involving the act at issue is brought to the court by a prosecutor or someone filing suit against another party. However, the essence of judicial review, as invented and practiced in the United States, is similar to constitutional review used in other democratic countries.

Several constitutional democracies, such as the Netherlands and Great Britain, do not practice judicial review. The rule of law is maintained in these countries through the democratic political process, especially elections, whereby the government is held accountable to the people. However, judicial review or constitutional review seems to be an especially strong means to protect the rights of minorities against the threat of oppression by a tyrannical majority of the people acting through its representatives in the government.

SEE ALSO Constitutionalism; Democracy, Representative and Constitutional; Justice; Majority Rule and Minority Rights; Rights; Rule of Law; Separation of Powers

Justice

Justice is one of the main goals of democratic constitutions, along with the achievement of order, security, liberty, and the common good. The Preamble to the Constitution of the United States, for example, says that one purpose of the document is to "establish Justice." And, in the 51st paper of *The Federalist*, James Madison proclaims, "Justice is the end of government. It is the end of civil society. It ever has been and ever will be pursued until it be obtained, or until liberty be lost in the pursuit." So, what is justice? And how is it pursued in a constitutional democracy?

Since ancient times, philosophers have said that justice is achieved when everyone receives what is due to her or him. Justice is certainly achieved when persons with equal qualifications receive equal treatment from the government. For example, a government establishes justice when it equally guarantees the human rights of each person within its authority. As each person is equal in her or his membership in the human species, each one possesses the same immutable human rights, which the government is bound to protect equally.

By contrast, the government acts unjustly if it protects the human rights of some individuals under its authority while denying the same protection to others. The racial segregation laws that prevailed in some parts of the United States until the mid-1960s, for example, denied justice to African American people. America's greatest civil rights leader, Martin Luther King Jr., said that racial segregation laws were "unjust laws" because they prevented black Americans from enjoying the same rights and opportunities as other citizens of the United States. When he opposed unjust racial segregation laws, King asserted that the worth and dignity of each person must be respected equally because each one is equally a member of the human species. Thus, any action by the government or groups of citizens that violated the worth and dignity of any person, as did the racial segregation laws, was unjust and should not be tolerated. King and his followers, therefore, protested these laws and eventually brought about their demise.

Another example of justice is *procedural justice*. It is pursued through *due process of law* to resolve conflicts between individuals or between individuals and their government. The government administers fair and impartial procedures equally to everyone under its authority in order to settle disputes among them or to prosecute persons charged with crimes against the state. For example, the 5th Amendment of the U.S. Constitution says that no person shall "be deprived of life, liberty, or property without due process of law, nor shall private property be taken for public use without just compensation." The 4th, 5th, and 6th Amendments include several guarantees of fair procedures for anyone accused of criminal behavior, including "the right to a speedy and public trial, by an impartial jury of the State and district wherein the crime shall have been committed."

When procedural due process prevails, conflicts are settled in an orderly and fair manner in a court of law, according to the rule of law, and not by the arbitrary actions of people in power. This equal justice under the law regulates the interactions among private individuals and between individuals and government. Punishments, such as incarceration in prison, payment of fines, or performance of community service, may be carried out against a wrongdoer. One party harmed by another may receive compensation from the perpetrator of the grievance.

Distributive justice, another type of justice pursued in every constitutional democracy, pertains to the government's enactment of laws to distribute benefits to the people under its authority. Distributive justice certainly is achieved when equals receive the same allocation of benefits. For example, public programs that provide social security or medical care to all elderly and retired persons are examples of distributive justice in a constitutional democracy. Public schools, which all children have an equal opportunity to attend, are another example.

When the government of a constitutional democracy protects individuals' rights to liberty, order, and safety, individuals can freely use their talents to produce wealth and enjoy the results of their labor. Thus, they are able to provide for their basic human needs and to satisfy many, if not all, of their wants. But some persons in every democracy are unable for various reasons to care adequately for themselves. Therefore, the government provides programs to distribute such basic benefits for disadvantaged persons as medical care, housing, food, and other necessities. These public programs for needy persons are examples of distributive justice in a constitutional democracy.

In the various democracies of our world, people debate the extent and kind of distributive justice there should be to meet adequately the social and economic needs of all the people. Should the regulatory power of government be increased greatly so that it can bring about greater social and economic equality through redistribution of resources?

Countries that provide extensive social and economic benefits through the redistribution of resources are known as social democracies or welfare states. The consequences of distributive justice in a social democracy, such as Sweden, are to diminish greatly unequal social and economic conditions and to move toward parity in general standards of living among the people.

However, the achievement of this kind of social justice requires a substantial increase in the power of government to regulate the society and economy. Thus, as social and economic equality increase through government intervention in the lives of individuals, there is a decrease in personal and private rights to freedom. People in democracies throughout the world debate whether justice is generally served or denied by big public programs that extensively redistribute resources in order to equalize standards of living among the people.

SEE ALSO Equality; Liberalism; Liberty; Rule of Law; Social Democracy

Liberalism

Liberalism is a theory of government that pertains to individuals' personal and private rights to liberty. In modern times, liberalism has been associated with a particular model of democracy that emphasizes limited government and the rule of law in order to secure the inherent and inalienable rights of individuals. The United States, the Czech Republic, Estonia, France, and the Slovak Republic are among the many constitutional democracies today that exemplify the defining characteristics of liberalism.

The essential characteristics of liberalism are beliefs or assumptions about the relationships of individuals, civil society, and government. They include the following ideas:

- the moral primacy of the individual against the claims of the state
- the equal moral worth and dignity of each person as a member of the human species
- the equal possession by each human being of inalienable natural rights, which include the individual's rights to life, liberty, and property
- the establishment of civil society and government in order to protect equally the inherent rights of each person
- the importance of tolerating individual differences and diversity in civic, political, and social life
- the ultimate and overriding value attached to respect for the equal worth and dignity of each person, which sets a limit to toleration; nothing should be tolerated that violates the worth and dignity of the autonomous individual

The liberal model of government was implied by the American Declaration of Independence of 1776. It boldly asserts:

> We hold these Truths to be self-evident, that
> all Men Are created equal, that they are
> endowed by their Creator with certain

unalienable rights, that among these are Life,
Liberty, and the Pursuit of Happiness—That
to secure these Rights, Governments are
instituted among Men, deriving their just
Powers from the Consent of the Governed,
that whenever any Form of Government
becomes destructive of these Ends it is the
Right of the People to alter or abolish it, and
to institute new Government, laying its
Foundation on such Principles, and organizing its Powers in such Form, as to them
shall seem most likely to Effect their Safety
and Happiness.

Ideas about liberalism put forth in the Declaration of Independence have influenced the establishment and maintenance
of *liberal democracy* in countries around the world.

More than two hundred years later, for example, the
constitution adopted by the Slovak Republic in 1992 expressed
similar liberal ideas about individual rights. Article 12 of the
Slovak constitution declares, "All human beings are free
and equal in dignity and rights. Their fundamental rights and
freedoms are inalienable, irrevocable, and absolutely perpetual.
Fundamental rights shall be guaranteed in the Slovak Republic
to every person."

In every liberal democracy, a free and open civil society
and a free and open market economy are necessities. The
spirit of liberalism prompts the people to voluntarily and
privately maintain the nongovernmental organizations of civil
society and the free enterprise of a market economic system.
These bastions of private resources are countervailing forces
against unconstitutional uses of governmental power that
might abridge or abolish the fundamental rights of the people.
Prominent among the fundamental rights of individuals are
certain private rights such as freedom of conscience, free
exercise of religion, private ownership and use of property,
freedom of association, and protection against unwarranted or
unreasonable government intrusion into one's home or other
private domains of the society.

The first concern in the liberal idea of justice is equal protection by the government of the inherent rights of each individual. Laws that violate the inherent and inalienable rights of individuals must be overturned in order for justice to prevail.

Classical or traditional liberalism has been concerned primarily with limiting the power of constitutional government in order to curtail its reach into the private and free spaces of a market economy and civil society. Thus, freedom of individual action is maximized, and the power of the state and government is minimized. Proponents of classical liberal ideas, who emphasize a minimal state and a maximal zone of individual liberty, are named *libertarians*, and their political philosophy is called *libertarianism*.

Classical liberalism's emphasis on limited government as the singular means to achieving personal liberty was challenged strongly in the 20th century by proponents of positive government action in support of the less advantaged members of society. The critics of traditional or classical liberalism argued that uneducated, ill, undernourished, or homeless persons could not properly make use of their constitutionally guaranteed civil liberties.

In the interest of maximizing liberty for everyone, rich and poor alike, the critics of classical liberalism called for an increase of government power to provide social and economic benefits—such as access to basic education, health care, job training, and so forth—to people in need. According to the new liberalism, positive government action to help the neediest members of society was a necessary component of justice in combination with constitutional guarantees of traditional civil liberties.

These critics of the older liberalism became known as *welfare state liberals*. Because they called for the government to promote social and political equality in tandem with personal liberty, they were distinguished from antiliberal groups that favored socialism, the comprehensive control and regulation of society by government on behalf of equality at the expense of traditional civil liberties. The new liberalism, based on the positive use of power through government to benefit the neediest members of society, was integrated more or less with the old liberalism in the late 20th-century model of liberal democracy.

In the United States staunch advocates of the old liberalism including libertarians have become known as *conservatives,* because they stress the preservation of traditional ideas about limited government and civil liberties anchored in the founding of the nation. They tend to occupy the "right" side of the political spectrum. Proponents of big government programs, which enable positive public actions in support of enhanced liberty and equality for needy persons, have appropriated the label of liberalism or positive liberalism. They tend to occupy the "left" side of the political spectrum.

SEE ALSO Civil Society; Constitutionalism; Equality; Justice; Liberty; Market Economy; Rights; Social Democracy; State

Liberty

A person who has liberty is free to make choices about what to do or what to say. A primary purpose of government in the United States and other constitutional democracies is to protect and promote the liberty of individuals. The Preamble to the U.S. Constitution proclaims that a principal reason for establishing the federal government is to "secure the Blessings of Liberty to ourselves and our Posterity." The Preamble to the 1992 Czech constitution also stresses liberty: "We, the citizens of the Czech Republic...in the spirit of the inviolable values of human dignity and liberty, as a homeland of equal, free, citizens...hereby adopt, through our freely elected representatives, the following Constitution of the Czech Republic."

The U.S. Constitution, the Czech constitution, and the constitutions of other democracies throughout the world include guarantees for the protection of fundamental *civil liberties,* such as freedom of speech and press, freedom of assembly and association, freedom to vote and otherwise participate in elections of representatives in government, freedom of conscience, free exercise of religion, and freedom from unwarranted invasions of one's home or other private spaces in society. These freedoms are called civil liberties because individuals enjoy them only within the context of civil society and constitutional government.

Civil liberty in a constitutional democracy means liberty under laws enacted by the elected representatives of the people. Rights to civil liberty are exercised, constrained, and protected by laws made through the free and fair procedures of democracy. Liberty is secured by limiting the power of government to prevent it from abusing the people's rights. But if the government has too little power, so that law and order break down, then liberties may be lost. Neither freedom of thought nor freedom of action is secure in a lawless and disorderly society.

Ordered liberty is the desirable condition in which both public order and personal liberty are maintained. But how can liberty and authority, freedom and power, be combined and balanced so that one does not predominate over the other? This was the basic problem of constitutional government that concerned the founders of the United States, and it has continued to challenge Americans as democracy has evolved and expanded throughout the history of their country. Early on, James Madison noted the challenges of ordered liberty in a 1788 letter to Thomas Jefferson: "It is a melancholy reflection that liberty should be equally exposed to danger whether the Government has too much or too little power; and that the line which divides these extremes should be so inaccurately defined by experience."

Madison noted the standing threat to liberty posed by insufficient constitutional limits on government. He also recognized that liberty carried to the extreme, as in a riot, is equally dangerous to the freedom and other rights of individuals. Constitutional democracy may provide both liberty and order, but the right mix of these two factors can be difficult to find and maintain.

There are two continuously challenging questions about liberty and order that every democracy must confront and resolve. First, at what point, and under what conditions, should the power of government be limited in order to protect individuals' rights to liberty against the threat of despotism? Second, at what point, and under what conditions, should expressions of individual liberty be limited by law in order to maintain public order and stability and to prevent the demise of constitutional democracy? Every country that strives to achieve or maintain democracy must resolve these questions about liberty and order.

SEE ALSO Constitutionalism; Democracy, Representative and Constitutional; Liberalism; Rights

Majority Rule and Minority Rights

The essence of democracy is majority rule, the making of binding decisions by a vote of more than one-half of all persons who participate in an election. However, constitutional democracy in our time requires majority rule with minority rights. Thomas Jefferson, third President of the United States, expressed this concept of democracy in 1801 in his First Inaugural Address. He said,

> All . . . will bear in mind this sacred principle,
> that though the will of the majority is in all
> cases to prevail, that will to be rightful must
> be reasonable; that the minority possess their
> equal rights, which equal law must protect
> and to violate would be oppression.

In every genuine democracy today, majority rule is both endorsed and limited by the supreme law of the constitution, which protects the rights of individuals. Tyranny by a minority over the majority is barred, but so is tyranny of the majority against minorities.

This fundamental principle of constitutional democracy, majority rule coupled with the protection of minority rights, is embedded in the constitutions of all genuine democracies today. The 1992 constitution of the Czech Republic, for example, recognizes the concepts of majority rule and minority rights. Article 6 says, "Political decisions shall stem from the will of the majority, expressed by means of a free vote. The majority's decisions must heed the protection of the minorities." The Czech constitution is filled with statements of guaranteed civil liberties, which the constitutional government must not violate and which it is empowered to protect.

Majority rule is limited in order to protect minority rights, because if it were unchecked it probably would be used to oppress persons holding unpopular views. Unlimited majority rule in a democracy is potentially just as despotic as the unchecked rule of an autocrat or an elitist minority political party.

In every constitutional democracy, there is ongoing tension between the contradictory factors of majority rule and minority rights. Therefore, public officials in the institutions of representative government must make authoritative decisions about two questions. When, and under what conditions, should the rule of the majority be curtailed in order to protect the rights of the minority? And, conversely, when, and under what conditions, must the rights of the minority be restrained in order to prevent the subversion of majority rule?

These questions are answered on a case-by-case basis in every constitutional democracy in such a way that neither majority rule nor minority rights suffer permanent or irreparable damage. Both majority rule and minority rights must be safeguarded to sustain justice in a constitutional democracy.

SEE ALSO Constitutionalism; Democracy, Representative and Constitutional; Equality; Justice; Liberalism; Liberty; Rights

Market Economy

Democracy has flourished only in countries with some form of market economy, an economic system based on rights to private property and free enterprise. Conversely, democracy has never existed in countries with a state-centric or command economy, in which the government controls most of the property and industries.

A market economy is a dynamic and flexible system for producing and distributing the goods and services that the people of a country need and want. For example, there are ongoing transactions at multiple marketplaces, where individuals may freely interact to make decisions about what to buy and sell. These free-flowing exchanges between buyers and sellers affect the prices of goods and the profits of producers and sellers, as well as the supply of and demand for goods and services.

A market economy involves competition among producers and sellers of goods and services, who strive to outdo one another in attracting buyers or consumers of their products. Consumers also compete with one another to buy scarce goods or services.

The right to own and use private property and other resources for personal and public benefit is an essential characteristic of a market economy. Producers and sellers of goods and services, for example, use their property, money, time, skill, and other resources to make and sell products that consumers want to buy.

Freedom of exchange at the market, like other social interactions in a constitutional and representative democracy, is regulated by the rule of law. Thus, individual rights to own and use private property and to make economic choices are protected by the constitutional government of a democracy. The government regulates economic activity within limits framed by the constitution, thereby maintaining the order, security, enterprise, and competition needed for the market economy to work as it should. Thus, a market economy exemplifies liberty under the rule of law.

In every democracy, the constitutional government regulates economic activity in response to the interests of the
people. The range of regulation in various democracies extends
from the highly regulated markets of the social democracy
model to the less regulated markets of the liberal model.
However, democracy—and the liberty associated with it—is
not possible under a state-centric system, where the economy
is controlled by the government and government officials
with virtually unlimited power direct a state-controlled, or
command, economy, the antithesis of the market system.

A prime example of the command economy was the
Union of Soviet Socialist Republics (USSR), which existed
from 1917 until 1991. Through their total control of the
production and distribution of goods and services, government
officials had the power to dominate the inhabitants of their
realm. And there were no effective limits on their power
to abuse individuals at odds with the government or to
deprive unpopular persons of their rights to liberty, equality
of opportunity, and even life.

The ultimate deficiency of the command economy, however, was its lack of productivity. Thus, the standard of living
for most people in the Soviet Union was very low.

In contrast, the market economy, with its private property
rights and relatively free choices, forms a material foundation
for constitutional democracy, liberty, and prosperity. The
people of such constitutional democracies such as the United
States of America, Japan, and the countries of the European
Union have the highest standards of living in the world.

SEE ALSO Constitutionalism; Justice; Liberalism; Pluralism;
Social Democracy

Parliamentary System

Countries around the world practice democracy through different types of institutions. However, most democracies in the world today use the parliamentary system as opposed to a presidential system like that used in the United States. A few examples among the many parliamentary democracies are Canada, Great Britain, Italy, Japan, Latvia, the Netherlands, and New Zealand.

Defining characteristics of the parliamentary system are the supremacy of the legislative branch within the three functions of government—executive, legislative, and judicial—and blurring or merging of the executive and legislative functions. The legislative function is conducted through a unicameral (one-chamber) or bicameral (two-chamber) parliament composed of members accountable to the people they represent. A prime minister and the ministers of several executive departments of the government primarily carry out the executive function.

The political party or coalition of parties that make up a majority of the parliament's membership select the prime minister and department ministers. The prime minister usually is the leader of the majority party, if there is one, or the leader of one of the parties in the ruling coalition. Some ceremonial executive duties are carried out by a symbolic head of state—a hereditary king or queen in a democratic constitutional monarchy, such as Great Britain, Japan, Norway, or Spain, or an elected president or chancellor in a democratic constitutional republic such as Germany, Italy, or Latvia. The judicial function typically is independent of the legislative and executive components of the system.

In a parliamentary system, laws are made by majority vote of the legislature and signed by the head of state, who does not have an effective veto power. In most parliamentary democracies, the head of state can return a bill to the legislative body to signify disagreement with it. But the parliament can override this "veto" with a simple majority vote.

In most parliamentary systems, there is a special constitutional court that can declare a law unconstitutional if it violates provisions of the supreme law of the land, the constitution. In a few parliamentary systems, such as Great Britain, New Zealand, and the Netherlands, there is no provision for constitutional or judicial review, and the people collectively possess the only check on the otherwise supreme legislature, which is to vote members of the majority party or parties out of office at the next election.

A parliamentary democracy is directly and immediately responsive to popular influence through the electoral process. Members of parliament may hold their positions during an established period between regularly scheduled elections. However, they can be turned out of office at any point between the periodic parliamentary elections if the government formed by the majority party loses the support of the majority of the legislative body. If the governing body, the prime minister and his cabinet of executive ministers, suffers a "no confidence" vote against it in the parliament, then it is dissolved and an election may be called immediately to establish a new parliamentary membership. A new prime minister and cabinet of executive ministers may be selected by newly elected members of the parliament.

A few parliamentary democracies function as semipresidential systems. They have a president, elected by direct vote of the people, who exercises significant foreign policy powers apart from the prime minister. They also have a constitutional court with strong powers of constitutional or judicial review. For example, the constitutional democracy of Lithuania is a parliamentary system with characteristics of a presidential system, such as a president of the republic who is directly elected by the people and who has significant powers regarding national defense, military command, and international relations.

Advocates of the parliamentary system claim it is more efficient than the presidential alternative because it is not encumbered by checks and balances among power-sharing departments, which usually slow down the operations of government and sometimes create paralyzing gridlocks. Further, in the parliamentary system, a government that has lost favor with the people can be voted out of office immediately. Advocates claim that by responding more readily to the will of the people the parliamentary system is more democratic than the presidential alternative. However, both parliamentary and presidential systems can be genuine democracies so long as they conform to the essential characteristics by which a democracy is distinguished from a nondemocracy, including constitutionalism, representation based on democratic elections, and guaranteed rights to liberty for all citizens.

SEE ALSO Accountability; Democracy, Representative and Constitutional; Judicial Independence; Judicial Review; Participation; Presidential System: Political Party; Separation of Powers

Participation

Participation by citizens in their civil society and government is a necessary, if not sufficient, condition of democracy. *Civic participation* refers to the voluntary activities of citizens in forming and sustaining independent nongovernmental organizations that contribute to the well-being of the community. *Political participation* pertains to the activities of individuals and groups aimed at influencing the public policy decisions of their government. Through their political participation, citizens prompt their representatives in government to be accountable to the people. Unless there is some significant level of free and independent participation by citizens in the work of their civil society and government, there cannot be an authentic democracy.

The most common form of political participation by citizens is voting in elections for their representatives in government. By voting for or against particular candidates or political parties, citizens signify their approval or rejection of their representatives' performances. Thus, participation in elections is one way citizens can make their government responsive and accountable to the people.

In some democracies, citizens use the *initiative* and *referendum* to participate with the legislature in making laws, under certain conditions specified by the constitution. The *initiative* is the right of citizens to propose a law or a constitutional amendment either directly for public vote, or via a vote of the legislature through the submission of a petition signed by a requisite number of eligible voters. Thus, the initiative is a means by which citizens can place items directly on the lawmaking agenda or force their representatives in government to consider the matter.

The *referendum* is the right of citizens to approve or reject a law that their legislature has enacted. If a requisite number of citizens sign and submit a petition to their government during a specified period before a law becomes operational, then it is placed before the voters in an election. If a majority votes against the proposition, then the law is rejected. In some democracies, amendments to the constitution cannot become operational unless they are approved by a majority of the citizens in a countrywide referendum.

The rights of initiative or referendum are included in the constitutions of some parliamentary democracies. For example, Article 68 of the constitution of Lithuania says, "Citizens of the Republic of Lithuania shall have the right of legislative initiative. A draft law may be submitted to the *Seimas* [parliament] by 50,000 citizens of the Republic of Lithuania who have the right to vote. The *Seimas* must consider this draft law." The constitution of Estonia provides the right of referendum in Article 105, which says,

> The *Riigikogu* [parliament] shall have the
> right to put draft laws or other national issues
> to a referendum. The decision of the people
> shall be determined by the majority of those
> who participate in the referendum. A law
> which has been adopted by referendum shall
> be immediately proclaimed by the President
> of the Republic.

The constitutions of many democracies, including that of the United States, do not include the rights of initiative and referendum. However, more than half of the 50 U.S. states have constitutions that provide either the referendum or initiative or both of these procedures.

In addition to voting for representatives in government and using the initiative and referendum, other kinds of political participation in a democracy include:

- working in an election campaign to support a political candidate or political party
- contacting a legislator in order to influence her or his decision about a public policy issue
- writing a letter to a newspaper or writing a blog to influence public opinion about an issue
- donating money to the election campaign of a candidate or a political party

- organizing or joining a lawful public demonstration to support or oppose a public policy option or decision
- supporting an interest group in order to promote particular public policies

Proponents of a *participatory model of democracy* advocate a high level of citizen participation in order to make sure that the government is responsive and accountable to the people it represents. They want citizens to be involved to the maximum extent in activities that might influence decisions in government in order to ensure that democracy is based on the will of the people. In particular, they favor constitutional provisions for citizens to participate directly in the legislative process, such as the initiative and referendum.

By contrast, some advocates of the *liberal model of democracy*, while supporting the political participation of citizens, are most concerned with establishing and maintaining constitutional protections for individuals' personal rights to seek fulfillment on their own terms. This approach may encourage citizens to emphasize private pursuits instead of intense political participation. Some advocates of the liberal model emphasize the individual's freedom to choose, without undue public pressure, the extent to which he or she will participate politically and civically. By contrast, advocates of the participatory model of democracy claim that intensive and continuous participation by citizens is the best means both to personal fulfillment and to promotion of the common good.

An ongoing question about democracy concerns the extent, intensity, and immediacy of participation that is necessary to make democracy work for the benefit of the people. If democracy is not extensively participatory, can it really be government of, by, and for the people? Or is a heavy reliance on the representatives of the people, who are judged periodically by citizens through public elections, sufficient to sustain an authentic constitutional democracy?

SEE ALSO Citizenship; Civil Society; Elections; Liberalism; Pluralism; Political Party; Popular Sovereignty; Republicanism; Rights

Pluralism

Pluralism in a democracy is the widespread distribution of political power and influence within the state and civil society. Individuals and groups can express different points of view freely, independently, and effectively in order to influence public opinion and the decisions of government.

One indicator of pluralism in a democracy is a variety of interest groups, which put forward in the public domain competing points of view about public issues and policies. An *interest group* is an independent, nongovernmental organization that puts pressure on government officials to make decisions that collectively favor the members of the group. Sometimes an interest group is called a *pressure group*, because of the intensity of its effort to influence government decisions.

Unlike a political party, an interest group neither nominates candidates for election to public office nor tries to win control of the government through the electoral process. However, interest groups do participate in election campaigns by supporting individual candidates and political parties that favor their point of view. Interest group members also use the mass media and face-to-face interactions with people to influence public opinion in favor of their positions on public issues.

Interest groups are formed in a democracy in order to represent and advance the competing interests of different segments of the society and economy. For example, in the United States, there are many interest groups that promote the viewpoints of particular industries, such as the producers or sellers of petroleum, firearms, timber, dairy products, and coal. Labor unions are interest groups that represent workers in various occupations. Still other interest groups address particular topical concerns such as environmental protection, conservation of natural resources, needs of consumers, and the rights of women.

Pluralism in a democracy is exhibited by the existence of multiple competing centers of power. Various nongovernmental organizations, including interest groups, compete to promote their particular goals and their different visions of the common good. These private organizations are subject to the rule of law under a constitution, but they are beyond the direct control of government officials.

By contrast, the robust pluralism of a constitutional democracy is weak or absent in nondemocratic systems. In a totalitarian regime, such as the defunct Soviet Union, pluralism is not permitted. It is against the law to form free and independent nongovernmental organizations. Civic and political participation is encouraged, but only on the restrictive terms of the ruling party, which controls all social organizations and political groups in its regime. Pluralism is also diminished under the authoritarian regimes in countries such as the Kingdom of Saudi Arabia and the Republic of Iran. Political and social groups, especially religious groups outside the Islamic mainstreams of these societies, are either outlawed, suppressed, or otherwise marginalized.

SEE ALSO Civil Society; Diversity; Political Party; Rights

Political Party

A political party in a democracy is an independent and freely formed organization that nominates candidates for positions in government with the purpose of winning elections in order to form or control the government. Competition between candidates and political factions or parties is an essential characteristic of a genuine constitutional democracy. If only one political party is permitted to function in a country, or if there is only one officially approved slate of candidates, then there is not a democracy.

During the period between elections in a democratic country, the political parties that failed to win control of the government are free to criticize or otherwise legally oppose the ideas of the ruling party or coalition of parties. Thus, they try to win support among voters that will enable them to win the next election. If opposition to the ruling party is silenced, then there is not a democracy.

In a few democracies, such as Great Britain and the United States of America, there are only two major political parties that compete to win control of the national government. In the United States, for example, there are the Democrats and the Republicans, and in Great Britain, the Conservative Party and the Labour Party. Minor parties may exist in a two-party system, but rarely does one or more of their candidates win a position in national government. From time to time, however, a major party will adopt ideas put forward by a minor party. Sometimes a minor party grows strong enough to replace one of the major parties in a two-party system. During the 20th century, for example, the Labour Party in Great Britain was a minor party that grew strong enough to replace the Liberal Party as one of the two major parties.

In most democracies, there is a multiple-party system; there are several major political parties whose candidates have a realistic chance to win election to the government, and there are many other minor parties that rarely if ever win representation in the government. For example, there are at least eight political parties that usually win seats in the parliament of Estonia. But Estonia also has more than 30 minor parties that typically do not attract enough voters to be represented at all in the parliament. Nonetheless, they are free to express their ideas in the continuing hope of winning greater support among the voters.

Multiple political party systems prevail in parliamentary democracies that use *proportional representation*. Under proportional representation, the members of parliament do not represent constituents in a particular district of the country. Instead, candidates run for office as members of their political party's slate or list of candidates, which represent the country as a whole and not a single constituency. Thus, voters cast their ballots for one party's list of candidates in preference to the lists of competing political parties. The number of seats that a party wins in the parliament is based on the percentage of votes cast for the party's list of candidates. For example, suppose there are one hundred members of the parliament. A political party that wins 16 percent of the votes will have 16 members in the parliament; another party that wins 25 percent of the votes will have 25 members of the legislative body.

In electoral systems based on proportional representation, there is usually a rule that in order to win at least one seat in the parliament, a party must win at least 5 percent of the total votes cast in the election. Thus, political parties with very little support cannot hope to be represented in the parliament. This rule enhances the possibility that one party or a coalition of only two or three parties will gain the majority of seats in the parliament necessary to form a government.

Two-party systems prevail in democracies with an electoral system based on single-representative districts, such as in the United States, Great Britain, and some other countries founded and formerly ruled by Britain, such as Australia, Canada, and New Zealand. The candidate for the legislative body (in Britain the House of Commons, in the U.S. the Congress) with a majority or plurality of votes cast in each electoral district wins the seat for that district. This system discourages multiple political parties from competing in the single-representative districts upon which the election is based because only the candidate with the most votes wins a seat in the legislature and the losing party or parties get no seats, as might be the case in the proportional representation system.

Some multiple-party democracies have an electoral system that is a mixture of two electoral systems: the proportional representation system and the single-representative district system. For example, Estonia's electoral system includes 12 districts from which about 33 of the 101 members of parliament are elected to represent the people residing in these districts. The remaining seats are filled by proportional representation based on ballots cast on a national basis for the different party lists. As a result, roughly one-third of the members in the Estonian parliament are elected from particular districts and about two-thirds represent the country at large.

In all genuine democracies, more than one political party has the constitutional right to compete periodically in elections in order to form and conduct the government. However, if genuine democracy would prevail, the winners of majority support among the people must respect equally and fairly the rights of parties in the minority.

SEE ALSO Accountability; Elections; Parliamentary System; Presidential System

Popular Sovereignty

Popular sovereignty is government based on consent of the people. The government's source of authority is the people, and its power is not legitimate if it disregards the will of the people. Government established by free choice of the people is expected to serve the people, who have sovereignty, or supreme power.

There are four ways that popular sovereignty is expressed in a democracy. First, the people are involved either directly or through their representatives in the making of a constitution. Second, the constitution made in the name of the people is ratified by a majority vote of the people or by representatives elected by the people. Third, the people are involved directly or indirectly in proposing and ratifying amendments to their constitution. Fourth, the people indicate support for their government when they vote in pubic elections, uphold the constitution and basic principles of their government, and work to influence public policy decisions and otherwise prompt their representatives in government to be accountable to them.

Popular sovereignty was asserted as a founding principle of the United States of America. The Declaration of Independence of 1776 asserts that legitimate governments are those "deriving their just Powers from the Consent of the Governed." Later, in 1787, the framers of the U.S. Constitution proclaimed popular sovereignty in the document's Preamble: "We the people of the United States . . . do ordain and establish this Constitution for the United States of America." Popular sovereignty was also expressed in Article 7 of the Constitution, which required that nine states approve the proposed framework of government before it could become the supreme law of the land. The people of the several American states chose representatives to ratifying conventions who freely decided to approve the Constitution in the name of those who elected them. Popular sovereignty was also included in Article 5 of the Constitution, which provides the means to amend the Constitution through the elected representatives of the people. Finally, popular sovereignty is reflected in two different parts of the Constitution that require members of Congress to be elected directly by the people: Article 1 pertaining to the House of Representatives and Amendment 17 concerning election of senators.

The founding of the United States and the framing of its Constitution heralded the idea of popular sovereignty as the standard by which popular government should be established and sustained. The American example, exceptional in the late 18th century, has become a world-class standard of legitimacy for governments in the 21st century. No country can realistically claim to be a democracy unless it proclaims constitutionally and implements functionally the principle of popular sovereignty.

This standard has been upheld in the constitutions of democratic nation-states today. For example, Article 2 of the 1993 constitution of the Czech Republic says, "All state power derives from the people. . . . The state power serves all citizens and can be exercised only in cases within the scope stipulated by law, and by means specified by law." The 1988 constitution of Brazil asserts in Article 1, "All power emanates from the people, who exercise it by means of elected representatives or directly as provided by the constitution." And Article 2 of the 1992 constitution of the Republic of Lithuania says, "The State of Lithuania shall be created by the people. Sovereignty shall be vested in the people." Further, Article 4 says, "The people shall exercise the supreme sovereign power vested in them either directly or through their democratically elected representatives."

Popular sovereignty as the legitimate source of authority in government has become so widely recognized among the democracies of our world that even nondemocracies try to claim it in order to justify their exercise of power. For example, the constitution of the People's Republic of China is, according to its preamble, established in the name of the people and "led by the working class and based on the alliance of the workers and peasants." In reality, the Communist Party of China has appropriated power for itself, which it exercises dictatorially to suppress any organized opposition to its authority. Although economic freedom has increased dramatically in China in recent years, the party still tightly controls political life.

SEE ALSO Accountability; Authority; Constitution; Constitutionalism; Democracy, Representative and Constitutional; Participation; Republic; Republicanism

Presidential System

Some representative and constitutional democracies have a presidential system of government, which is based on the separation and sharing of powers among three independent and coordinate branches of government: legislative, executive, and judicial.

The United States is the originator and primary example of the presidential system, a model that is followed in only a few other democracies, such as Argentina, Brazil, Mexico, and the Philippines.

The presidential system, unlike the parliamentary form of democracy, has a strong and independent chief executive with extensive powers related to both domestic, or internal, affairs and foreign policy. The president's independence from the legislature is based on election by the people to whom he or she is directly accountable and not to the legislature, as in the parliamentary system. Furthermore, the constitution grants strong powers to the chief executive in a presidential system.

In the 70th paper of *The Federalist*, Alexander Hamilton argued for a strong Presidency, as provided by the U.S. Constitution. He wrote,

> Energy in the executive is a leading character in the definition of good government. It is essential to the protection of the community against foreign attacks: it is not less essential to the steady administration of the laws; to the protection of property . . . [and] to the security of liberty against the enterprises and assaults of ambition, of faction, and of anarchy.

In the U.S. presidential system, the President is both the chief executive of the government and the head of state. The President oversees the executive branch of government, which includes the cabinet, or heads of various executive departments, and various administrative bureaus and agencies. The chief executive and the subordinate executive officers have the power and duty to carry out and enforce laws and to administer the day-to-day business of the government. In particular, the President commands the armed forces and is responsible for the defense of the country against internal disorder and foreign attack.

The separate and independent legislative and judicial branches of government, which share power with the executive, prevent the strong executive authority of the presidential system of democracy from becoming excessive or abusive. The bicameral Congress, consisting of the House of Representatives and Senate, is the legislative or law-making branch of government in the United States. The judicial branch, which interprets and applies the law in specific cases, includes the Supreme Court, intermediate appellate courts, and district courts at the entry level of jurisdiction.

There are *checks and balances* among the three separate branches of government, which prevent any one branch from continuously dominating the government, as the legislature does in the parliamentary system of democracy. For example, the U.S. Congress makes laws by majority vote of both its houses, and the President can veto these legislative acts. But the Congress can override a Presidential veto by a supermajority vote of two-thirds of the members of each house. The Supreme Court can use its power of judicial review in cases brought before it in order to decide whether the actions of the executive and legislative branches conform to the Constitution. If the Court rules they do not, then the Court can nullify them. There are many other examples in the U.S. Constitution of the separation of powers and checks and balances among the three branches of government.

By contrast with a parliamentary democracy, which permits elections whenever the government loses majority support in the parliament, elected officials in a presidential system serve strictly established terms of office. In the United States, for example, the President serves for four years, members of the Senate for six, and members of the House of Representatives for two. Members of the United States federal judiciary serve lifetime appointments, unless they choose to retire from office.

In the United States, the President, other executive officers, and members of the judiciary can be dismissed through a constitutionally prescribed process of impeachment and conviction, but this has happened only rarely. Members of Congress may force their peers from office for unethical or criminal behavior. This, too, has occurred infrequently. Usually, citizens have no way to force an unpopular President out of power or change the membership of Congress in advance of regularly scheduled elections. Thus, the leading legislative and executive officials in a presidential system of democracy are less immediately accountable to the people than are those in a parliamentary system.

The constitution of Argentina provides a presidential system very similar to that of the United States. The citizens directly elect the president to a six-year term of office. The constitution grants to the chief executive strong powers similar to those of the United States President. There is a system of checks and balances among three independent branches of government, very similar to that of the United States, which prevents the strong presidency from exercising power abusively or arbitrarily.

Advocates of the presidential system of democracy claim that it is more stable than the parliamentary alternative. They also say that its complex mechanisms of separated and shared powers, checks and balances, require far more deliberation and compromise of different interests in making laws than occurs in the parliamentary system, thus improving the quality of legislation. Finally, supporters of the presidential form of democracy argue that through separation of powers with checks and balances among the coordinate branches, the presidential system is the best way to achieve limited government and protection of individual rights, especially the rights of minorities.

SEE ALSO Accountability; Democracy, Representative and Constitutional; Judicial Independence; Judicial Review; Parliamentary System: Political Party; Separation of Powers

Republic

A republic is a form of government based on the consent of the people and operated by representatives elected by the people. Hereditary rule by a monarchy or an aristocratic class is prohibited.

Most democracies in the world today style themselves as republics or democratic republics. For example, Article 1 of the 1988 constitution of the Republic of Korea (South Korea) declares, "The Republic of Korea shall be a democratic republic. The sovereignty of the Republic of Korea shall reside in the people, and all state authority shall emanate from the people." And the 1948 constitution of the Republic of Italy says in Article 1, "Italy is a democratic republic founded on labor. The sovereignty belongs to the people who exercise it in accordance with the procedures and within the limits laid down by the constitution."

However, not all democracies are republics, and not all republics are democracies. For example, the United Kingdom, one of the leading democracies of the world, is not a republic but a constitutional monarchy. Other prominent constitutional monarchies that are authentic democracies include Denmark, Japan, the Netherlands, Norway, Spain, and Sweden. The defunct Union of Soviet Socialist Republics (the Soviet Union) consisted of 15 constituent socialist republics of which the Soviet Socialist Republic of Russia was most prominent. However, the Soviet Union did not fulfill the criteria by which democracy is defined among the countries of our world. Likewise, the current communist states of China, Cuba, and North Korea are nondemocractic republics because they neither conduct democratic elections nor justly protect the rights of particular minorities.

Prominent among the nondemocratic republics of the world today are such authoritarian or despotic countries as Algeria, Angola, Burma (Myanmar), Iran, Libya, Pakistan, Sudan, Syria, Uzbekistan, and Zimbabwe. In some nondemocratic republics, such as Iran, there are periodic elections of representatives to a parliament that makes laws by majority vote of the members. However, because there is majority rule without adequate protection of minority rights, elections are not sufficiently inclusive, and all groups in the country do not possess citizenship on equal terms.

The founders of the United States proclaimed their country to be a republic. And Article 4, Section 4 of the U.S. Constitution promised that every state within the country would be a republic. It says, "The United States [federal government] shall guarantee to every State in this Union a Republican Form of Government." Article 1, Section 9 emphatically disassociates the United States of America from any form of aristocracy or hereditary nobility. It says, "No title of Nobility shall be granted by the United States: And no Person holding any Office of Profit or Trust under them, shall without the Consent of the Congress, accept of any present, Emolument, Office, or title, of any kind whatever, from any King, Prince, or foreign State."

In the 39th paper of *The Federalist,* written in 1788, James Madison explained the idea of a republic or republican form of government that is embodied in the U.S. Constitution. He wrote,

> What, then, are the distinctive characters of the republican form? . . . If we resort for a criterion . . . we may define a republic to be . . . a government which derives all its powers directly or indirectly from the great body of the people, and is administered by persons holding their offices during pleasure for a limited period, or during good behavior. It is essential to such a government that it be derived from the great body of the society, not from an inconsiderable proportion or a favored class of it. . . . It is sufficient for such a government that the persons administering it be appointed either directly or indirectly by the people; and that they hold their appointments by either of the tenures just specified.

In the world of the 1770s and 1780s, such a republican form of government was rare; hereditary monarchies and aristocracies prevailed. These non-republican forms of government functioned without representation of or participation by the common people. Unlike most peoples of the world in the late 18th century, Americans were committed to representative, popular, and free government based on the consent of the governed. They established constitutional and representative government in their republic, the United States of America, which is the foundation of democracy in that country today.

SEE ALSO Authority; Democracy, Representative and Constitutional; Popular Sovereignty; Republicanism

Republicanism

Republicanism is a theory of government that emphasizes the participation of citizens for the common good of the community. The responsibilities and duties of citizens are paramount, and the exemplary citizen readily subordinates personal to public interests. In contrast to liberalism, which is concerned primarily with the personal and private rights of individuals, republicanism stresses the public rights and obligations of citizens to cooperate in support of their community.

Essential characteristics of republicanism are beliefs or assumptions about the relationships of individuals, the community, and government, including the following ideas:

- the needs of the community are considered superior to the claims of the individual
- citizens are obligated to participate extensively and cooperatively in public affairs
- the common civic identity is primary over diverse and particular identities
- political and civic unity are valued more than diversity or pluralism in the community
- citizens are equal in their duties, responsibilities, and rights
- participation by citizens is the means to accountability in government and to personal fulfillment
- popular sovereignty is the foundation of good government
- good government carries out the general will of the people
- all citizens are capable of self-rule
- all citizens are capable of civic virtue and are obligated to cultivate it
- good republican government depends upon the continuous civic and political participation of virtuous citizens

Republicanism is rooted in the political and civic ideas of classical antiquity, as they were expressed and practiced in the city-communities of Greece and in the Republic of Rome. These ideas were revived during the Renaissance era in western Europe, particularly in the city-based republics of northern Italy, such as Florence, Genoa, and Venice. Leading French philosophers of the European Enlightenment, such as Montesquieu and Jean-Jacques Rousseau, also put forward republican political ideas.

By contrast, the political philosophy of liberalism, based on the primacy of constitutionally guaranteed rights of individuals, is distinctly modern. Prominent among the formulators of liberal political ideas during and after the Enlightenment era were the English political philosophers John Locke and John Stuart Mill.

The founders of the United States of America combined ideas of republicanism and liberalism in their establishment of a constitutional government designed to guarantee the inherent and inalienable rights of individuals. The founding era produced a hybrid theory of liberal republicanism that developed into the democratic republic of the United States of America and subsequently influenced the worldwide spread of representative and constitutional democracy.

Proponents of the participatory model of democracy emphasize republicanism more than liberalism, but both systems of political thought have a place in their ideas about good government. Conversely, advocates of the liberal model of democracy recognize the importance of political and civic participation for the common good, but they subordinate it to the personal and private rights of individuals. There is an ongoing debate among promoters of representative and constitutional democracy about the appropriate blend of these two strains of political thought in the institutions of government and the public life of citizens.

SEE ALSO Accountability; Citizenship; Democracy, Representative and Constitutional; Liberalism; Participation; Republic; Virtue, Civic

Rights

The constitution of a democracy guarantees the rights of the people. A right is a person's justifiable claim, protected by law, to act or be treated in a certain way. For example, the constitutions of democracies throughout the world guarantee the political rights of individuals, such as the rights of free speech, press, assembly, association, and petition. These rights must be guaranteed in order for there to be free, fair, competitive, and periodic elections by the people of their representatives in government, which is a minimal condition for the existence of a democracy. If a democracy is to be maintained from one election to the next, then the political rights of parties and persons outside the government must be constitutionally protected in order for there to be authentic criticism and opposition of those in charge of the government. Thus, the losers in one election can use their political rights to gain public support and win the next election.

In addition to political rights, the constitutions of democracies throughout the world protect the rights of people accused of crimes from arbitrary or abusive treatment by the government. Individuals are guaranteed due process of law in their dealings with the government. Today, constitutional democracies protect the personal and private rights of all individuals under their authority. These rights include

- freedom of conscience or belief
- free exercise of religion
- privacy in one's home or place of work from unwarranted or unreasonable intrusions by the government
- ownership and use of private property for personal benefit
- general freedom of expression by individuals, so long as they do not interfere with or impede unjustly the freedom or well-being of others in the community

A turning point in the history of constitutionally protected rights was the founding of the United States of America in the late 18th century. The United States was born with a

Declaration of Independence that proclaimed as a self-evident truth that every member of the human species was equal in possession of "certain unalienable rights" among which are the rights to "Life, Liberty, and the Pursuit of Happiness."

The founders declared that the primary reason for establishing a government is "to secure these rights." And, if governments would act legitimately to protect the rights of individuals, then they must derive "their just Powers from the Consent of the Governed." Further, if the government established by the people fails to protect their rights and acts abusively against them, then "it is the Right of the People to alter or to abolish it, and to institute new Government" that will succeed in fulfilling its reason for existence—the protection of individual rights

Ideas expressed in the Declaration of Independence about rights and government were derived from the writings of political philosophers of the European Enlightenment, especially those of the Englishman John Locke. Enlightenment philosophers stressed that rights belonged equally and naturally to each person because of their equal membership in the human species. According to Locke, for example, persons should not believe that the government granted their rights, or that they should be grateful to the government for them. Instead, they should expect government to protect these equally possessed rights, which existed prior to the establishment of civil society and government. Thus, the rights of individuals, based on the natural equality of human nature, were called *natural rights.*

This Declaration of Independence, based on this natural rights philosophy, explained to the world that Americans severed their legal relationship with the United Kingdom because the mother country had violated the rights of the people in her North American colonies. As a result, the Americans declared they would independently form their own free government to protect their natural rights. In 1787, the Americans framed a constitution to "secure the Blessings of Liberty" and fulfill the primary purpose of any good government as expressed in the Declaration of Independence, the protection of natural rights, and they ratified this Constitution in 1788.

In 1789, the U.S. Congress proposed constitutional amendments to express explicitly the rights of individuals that the government was bound to secure; in 1791, the requisite number of states ratified 10 of these amendments, which became part of the U.S. Constitution. Thus, the American Bill of Rights was born. Since then, the American Bill of Rights has been an example and inspiration to people throughout the world who wish to enjoy liberty and equality in a constitutional democracy.

Following the tragedies of World War II, which involved gross abuses by some governments and their armies—Nazi Germany and imperial Japan, for example—against millions of individuals and peoples of the world, there was a worldwide movement in favor of the idea of human rights. The United Nations, an organization of the world's nation-states established after World War II in order to promote international peace and justice, became a leader in the promotion of human rights throughout the world. In 1948, this international body issued the United Nations Universal Declaration of Human Rights, which is a statement of the rights every human being should have in order to achieve a minimally acceptable quality of life.

Its first article says, "All human beings are born free and equal in dignity and rights. They are endowed with reason and conscience and should act toward one another in a spirit of brotherhood." Article 2 continues, "Everyone is entitled to all the rights and freedoms set forth in this Declaration, without distinction of any kind, such as race, color, sex, language, religion, political or other opinion, national or social origin, property, birth or other status." The remainder of the document details the human rights that ideally should be enjoyed by each person in the world.

Since 1948, the United Nations has issued several other documents on human rights, such as the International Covenant on Economic, Social, and Cultural Rights and the International Covenant on Civil and Political Rights. The

UN documents are statements of ideals about human rights intended to guide the actions of the world's nation-states, but the United Nations cannot enforce them in the way that a sovereign nation-state can compel obedience to laws within its territory. Thus, practical protection for human rights is possible today only through the governmental institutions of the world's independent nation-states. The quality of the protection of human rights varies significantly from country to country. It depends upon what the nation's constitution says about rights and the capacity of the government to enforce the rights guaranteed in its constitution.

There is general international agreement that there are two basic categories of human rights. First, there are rights pertaining to what should not be done to any human being. Second, there are rights pertaining to what should be done for every human being.

The first category of human rights involves constitutional guarantees that prohibit the government from depriving people of some political or personal rights. For example, the government cannot constitutionally take away someone's right to participate freely and independently in an election or to freely practice a particular religion. The second category of human rights requires positive action by the government to provide someone with a social or economic right that otherwise would not be available to her or him. Thus, the government may be expected to provide opportunities for individuals to go to school or to receive healthcare benefits.

The constitutions of many democracies specify certain social and economic rights that the government is expected to provide. In other democracies, for example the United States, programs that provide social and economic rights or entitlements, such as social security benefits for elderly persons and medical care for indigent persons, are established through legislation that is permitted but not required by the constitution.

SEE ALSO Equality; Justice; Liberalism; Liberty; Social Democracy

Rule of Law

In a limited government administered according to the rule of law, the rulers use power following established principles and procedures based on a constitution. By contrast, when the rulers wield power capriciously, there is rule by the unbridled will of individuals without regard for established law. The rule of law is an essential characteristic of every constitutional democracy that guarantees rights to liberty. It prevails in the government, civil society, and market economy of every state with a functional constitution.

The rule of law exists when a state's constitution functions as the supreme law of the land, when the statutes enacted and enforced by the government invariably conform to the constitution. For example, the second clause of Article 6 of the U.S. Constitution says,

> This Constitution, and the Laws of the United States which shall be made in Pursuance thereof; and all Treaties made, or which shall be made, under the Authority of the United States, shall be the supreme Law of the land; and the Judges in every State shall be bound thereby, anything in the Constitution or Laws of any State to the Contrary notwithstanding.

The third clause of Article 6 says, "The Senators and Representatives before mentioned and the Members of the several State Legislatures, and all executive and judicial Officers, both of the United States and of the several States, shall be bound by Oath or Affirmation to support this Constitution." These statements about constitutional supremacy have been functional throughout the history of the United States, which is the reason that the rule of law has prevailed from the country's founding era until the present.

The rule of law, however, is not merely rule by law; rather, it demands equal justice for each person under the authority of a constitutional government. So, the rule of law exists in a democracy or any other kind of political system only when the following standards are met:

- laws are enforced equally and impartially
- no one is above the law, and everyone under the authority of the constitution is obligated equally to obey the law
- laws are made and enforced according to established procedures, not the rulers' arbitrary will
- there is a common understanding among the people about the requirements of the law and the consequences of violating the law
- laws are not enacted or enforced retroactively
- laws are reasonable and enforceable

There is a traditional saying about the rule of law in government: "It is a government of laws and not of men and women." When the rule of law prevails in a democracy, there is equal justice and ordered liberty in the lives of the people. In this case, there is an authentic constitutional democracy. When rule of law does not prevail, there is some form of despotism in which power is wielded arbitrarily by a single person or party.

SEE ALSO Constitutionalism; Government, Constitutional and Limited

Separation of Powers

The separation of powers among three independent branches of government is a defining characteristic of the presidential system that characterizes the institutions of some constitutional democracies, such as Argentina, Brazil, Panama, the Philippines, and the United States of America. The U.S. Constitution is the original functional model for separation of powers among the legislative, executive, and judicial branches of government.

The legislative branch of the U.S. government, Congress, has the power, according to Article 1 of the Constitution, to make certain kinds of laws. In Article 2, the Constitution says that the executive branch, headed by the President, has the power to enforce or carry out laws. The judicial branch, headed by the Supreme Court, is established in Article 3 of the Constitution to interpret and apply the laws in court cases that come before it. Further, the first article of the Constitution divides legislative power between the two houses of Congress, the Senate and the House of Representatives. A majority vote in both houses is required for a bill to become law.

The Constitution provides to each branch of the government means to share in the power of the other branches. The mechanisms by which the three separate branches are able to restrain the others are called *checks and balances*.

There are several ways that one branch of the government checks the actions of another branch to maintain a balance of powers, so that no branch can dominate the others. The President, the chief of the executive branch, can check Congress by vetoing bills it has passed. But the President's veto can be overturned by a subsequent two-thirds vote of both houses of Congress. The President appoints executive branch officials and federal judges, including Justices of the Supreme Court. But the Senate, one part of the legislative branch, must approve the President's appointments by a majority vote; if not, the President's appointments are rejected.

The President is the commander in chief of the armed forces. But only Congress can enact legislation to provide funds to the armed forces and their commanders for their military operations. The Constitution grants power to the President to make treaties with foreign governments, but the Senate has power to confirm or reject them. Additional examples of the separation and sharing of powers among the executive and legislative branches, involving checks and balances, are found in Articles 1 and 2 of the Constitution.

The judicial branch of government uses its power to interpret the Constitution and the laws made under it in order to check the other two branches of government and to maintain the separation of powers among the three branches. For example, the Supreme Court uses judicial review to prevent either the legislative or executive branch from violating the Constitution. The Court can declare null and void actions of the Congress or the President that exceed or contradict their powers as expressed in the Constitution.

The principle of judicial independence, established in Article 3 of the Constitution, prevents the other two branches from intimidating the judicial branch and impeding it from properly checking them if they overstep their constitutional boundaries. The Constitution provides for lifetime terms of office and prohibits Congress from punishing judges by reducing the level of payment for their services in order to buttress the judicial branch's independence.

Separation and sharing of powers among the three branches, through checks and balances, is the basic constitutional means for achieving limited government and thereby protecting the people from governmental abuses. Each branch of a constitutional government has some influence over the actions of the others, but no branch can exercise its powers without cooperation from the others. The constitution of a presidential democracy prevents any one branch from encroaching upon the domains of the other branches.

Under the system of checks and balances, no branch of the government can accumulate too much power. But each branch, and the government generally, is supposed to have enough power to do what the people expect of it. So, the government is both limited and empowered; neither too strong for survival of the people's liberty nor too limited to be effective in maintaining order, stability, and security for the people.

During the founding era of the United States, James Madison expressed the importance of separated powers in a constitutional government. In the 47th paper of *The Federalist,* Madison wrote, "The accumulation of all powers, legislative, executive and judiciary, in the hands of one, a few, or many, and whether hereditary, self-appointed, or elected, may justly be pronounced the very definition of tyranny." In the next *Federalist* paper, Madison cautioned that unless the separate branches of government "be so far connected and blended [balanced] as to give each a constitutional control [check] over the others the degree of separation . . . essential to a free government can never in practice be duly maintained."

The parliamentary system of constitutional democracy also includes a distribution of powers in government among the legislative, executive, and judicial functions. The parliament enacts the laws, and the executive officers of the government, the prime minister in tandem with the various ministers of executive departments, execute the laws. However, the prime minister and other executive ministers derive their authority from the parliament and are answerable to it. In most parliamentary systems, there is an independent judiciary department that can declare null and void acts of the parliament or the executive ministers that violate the constitution. However, the parliamentary form of constitutional democracy is not based on a strict system of separated and shared powers.

Advocates of parliamentary democracy claim that it is more efficient than the presidential system, and that it is more responsive to the will of the people. They assert that the complex system of checks and balances among three separate and independent branches of government slows down decision making and sometimes thwarts the will of the majority of citizens, instead of directly and readily expressing it.

Defenders of separated and shared powers emphasize the importance of deliberate decision making in support of their system of constitutional democracy. They believe that the compromises necessary to achieve agreement among different groups empowered with checks on the actions of the other groups result in a government that cannot act recklessly.

Justice Louis D. Brandeis of the U.S. Supreme Court nicely summed up the justification for separated and shared powers in the Constitution. In his dissenting opinion in the 1926 case *Myers* v. *United States*, Justice Brandeis wrote,

> The doctrine of the separation of powers was adopted by the Convention of 1787, not to promote efficiency but to preclude the exercise of arbitrary power. The purpose was not to avoid friction but, by means of the inevitable friction incident to the distribution of the governmental powers among three departments, to save the people from autocracy.

SEE ALSO Constitutionalism; Government, Constitutional and Limited; Judicial Independence; Judicial Review; Parliamentary System; Presidential System

Social Democracy

Social democracy is a system of political thought and action that calls upon the government to provide certain social and economic rights or entitlements necessary to the well-being of all members of the community. Social democratic parties promote it in constitutional democracies throughout the world, but especially in Europe, where the social democracy movement was born.

Social democratic political parties try to mobilize political support for positive state and government actions. They aim to provide such social and economic rights as equal opportunities for basic education, adequate health care, acceptable housing, productive employment in the workforce, fair payment for workers, and guaranteed pension plans for people retired from the workforce. Social democrats claim that their commitment to social and economic rights in addition to traditional liberal ideas about political and private rights is an advanced or more fully developed model of democracy in comparison with the liberal model. While the traditional liberal model of democracy only emphasizes individual liberty, the social democratic model, according to its proponents, stresses both liberal and egalitarian ideals.

Several constitutional democracies in Europe—Denmark, Norway, and Sweden, for example—and elsewhere include significant social democratic parties, which campaign to promote egalitarian policies in the government. India is a prominent representative and constitutional democracy with a very strong commitment to the ideals of social democracy. The preamble to the 1950 constitution of India says the political system is "a sovereign socialist secular democratic republic" and providing certain egalitarian social and economic rights is proclaimed to be a responsibility of the state to its people.

By contrast with some of the constitutional democracies in Europe, the United States of America has not had a strong social democracy movement. There has never been a major political party in the United States that has styled itself as social democratic. The Democratic Party has been more accepting than its Republican rival of ideas associated with social democracy or welfare state liberalism. However, both major political parties in the United States have maintained their primary commitments to the liberal model of democracy, and have avoided identification with full-blown social democracy. The parties tend to justify their legislatively enacted programs of social and economic entitlements as government action in response to the wishes of constituents, not as constitutionally mandated rights.

Critics of social democracy in the United States and elsewhere stress that a very strongly empowered state and government is required to carry out the social democracy program of social and economic rights. The critics claim that positive state action to provide egalitarian social programs requires extensive redistribution of wealth and excessive government regulation of the society and economy. Thus, advocates of individual rights associated with the traditional liberal model of democracy claim that their principles of liberty would be minimized or even sacrificed if the egalitarian ideals of social democracy were to be maximized through excessive control of society by the government.

SEE ALSO Common Good; Equality; Justice; Liberalism; Liberty; Republicanism

State

A state is a political community occupying a specific territory that claims sovereignty or independence in the exercise of power over the people of its territory. The state or nation-state is the basic political unit of the international community. The United Nations is an international organization that includes 191 states or nation-states. A state may also refer to the subordinate political units of a federal system, such as the 50 states of the United States of America.

The state includes all the political or governmental institutions that collectively exercise legitimate power over the people in a particular territory. More than half the states or nation-states of the world today can realistically claim to have crossed the threshold to democracy. They have met the minimal standards by which a democracy is distinguished from a nondemocracy.

Among the most unfree and nondemocratic states of the world today are the few remaining communist regimes, such as China, Cuba, North Korea, and Vietnam. Other prominent examples of unfree and nondemocratic states are Burma (Myanmar), Guinea, Syria, and Zimbabwe. Individual dictators or a single political party rule these states autocratically or despotically with little or no accountability to the people under their control and little or no restraint by the constitution or laws of the land. By contrast, the free and democratic states, while claiming sovereignty and independence relative to other nation-states of the international community, recognize that popular sovereignty, the consent of the people, is the source of governmental authority in the democratic nation-state.

SEE ALSO Authority; Citizen; Citizenship; Federalism; Unitary State

Unitary State

In a unitary state, the central or national government has complete authority over all other political divisions or administrative units. For example, the Republic of France is a unitary state in which the French national government in Paris has total authority over several provinces, known as departments, which are the subordinate administrative components of the nation-state. The local governments of a unitary state carry out the directives of the central government, but they do not act independently.

The federal system of political organization is the exact opposite of the unitary state. For example, in contrast to the unitary state of France, Germany is a federal republic, which means that the national or federal government in Berlin shares political authority with the governments of several *Lander,* or political units within the nation-state. However, as in all federal states, including Australia, India, and the United States of America, the central or national government of Germany is supreme within the sphere of authority granted to it through the constitution.

Unitary states, like federal states, can be constitutional democracies or unfree nondemocracies. Both the unitary Republic of France and the Federal Republic of Germany, for example, are constitutional democracies, but the unitary states of Algeria, Libya, and Swaziland are unfree nondemocracies. The Republic of the Sudan is an example of an unfree and nondemocratic federal state.

SEE ALSO Federalism; State; Republic

Virtue, Civic

Virtue is excellence in the character of a person. It refers to a desirable disposition, which can prompt individuals to be good persons and to do good things in regard to others and the community in general. Civic virtue refers to the dispositions or habits of behavior that direct citizens to subordinate their personal interests when necessary to contribute significantly to the common good of their community.

Since ancient times, political philosophers have stressed the importance of civic virtue in the establishment and maintenance of good government. For example, Aristotle, the great philosopher of ancient Greece, identified four main virtues that a good citizen of a republic should exhibit: temperance (meaning self-restraint); prudence; fortitude; and justice.

Political thinkers and actors in modern times have also emphasized the importance of civic virtue in the character of the citizens and the institutions of a constitutional democracy or democratic republic. They have recognized that the practical effectiveness of constitutionalism—limited government and the rule of law—is dependent upon the character of the people. After all, in a democracy—government of, by, and for the people—the quality of constitutionalism can be no better than the character of the people. For example, citizens who possess the civic virtue of temperance are habitually disposed to limit their behavior and respect the rule of law, and to influence others to do the same.

Citizens who have cultivated the virtue of fortitude are likely to oppose persistently and strenuously government officials who behave corruptly or unconstitutionally, and to encourage other citizens to do likewise. Citizens who have learned the virtue of prudence are inclined to deliberation and reflection in making decisions rather than to reckless and destructive action, and they influence other citizens by the excellence of their civic behavior. Citizens with a well-formed sense of justice are habitually disposed to support community-wide standards for the protection of human rights and the promotion of the common good, and to prompt others to behave similarly. The core civic virtues are integrated within the character of the good citizen, who brings them in concert with other citizens of similar disposition to civic and political participation in a constitutional democracy.

During the founding of the United States of America, James Madison noted the close connection between civic morality and good constitutional government in a republic. In a speech at the Virginia Convention to ratify the U.S. Constitution, Madison said, "Is there no virtue among us? If there be not . . . no theoretical checks, no form of government can render us secure. To suppose that any form of government will secure liberty or happiness without any virtue in the people is a chimerical [unrealistic] idea."

Later, the French political philosopher Alexis de Tocqueville concurred with Madison in his great book *Democracy in America*. Tocqueville observed how the good character of citizens buttressed the institutions of constitutional government, enabling democracy to succeed in the United States during the 1830s. He recognized that if most citizens in the community have learned certain "habits of the heart" or civic virtues compatible with constitutionalism then there will be good constitutional government in a democracy. If not, however, even the most adroitly designed constitution, institutions of government, and statutes will fail to yield the desired results of liberty, order, and equal justice under law.

Democracy is not a self-sufficient system of government. It is a way of political and civic life that can thrive only among people with sufficient virtue to nurture and sustain it.

SEE ALSO Citizenship; Constitutionalism; Justice; Participation

FURTHER READING

Crick, Bernard. *Democracy: A Very Short Introduction*. Oxford, U.K.: Oxford University Press, 2002.

Dahl, Robert A. *On Democracy*. New Haven, Conn.: Yale University Press, 1998.

Gordon, Scott. *Controlling the State: Constitutionalism from Ancient Athens to Today*. Cambridge, Mass.: Harvard University Press, 1999.

Hamilton, Alexander, James Madison, and John Jay. *The Federalist*. Ed. Charles Kessler and Clinton Rossiter. New York: Mentor, 1999.

Huntington, Samuel P. *The Third Wave: Democracy in the Late Twentieth Century*. Norman: University of Oklahoma Press, 1991.

Perry, Michael. *The Idea of Human Rights*. New York: Oxford University Press, 1998.

Putnam, Robert D. *Making Democracy Work: Civic Traditions in Modern Italy*. Princeton, N.J.: Princeton University Press, 1993.

Riesenberg, Peter. *Citizenship in the Western Tradition*. Chapel Hill: University of North Carolina Press, 1992.

Sartori, Giovanni. *The Theory of Democracy Revisited*. Chatham, N.J.: Chatham House, 1987.

Tocqueville, Alexis de. *Democracy in America*. Ed. Harvey Mansfield and Delba Winthrop. Chicago: University of Chicago Press, 2000.

Touraine, Alain. *What Is Democracy?* Boulder, Colo.: Westview, 1997.

Woodruff, Paul. *First Democracy: The Challenge of an Ancient Idea*. New York: Oxford University Press, 2005.

WEBSITES

Albert Shanker Institute
www.ashankerinst.org

This organization promotes discussions and sponsors research on challenges facing the democracies of our world. This site includes position papers on education for democracy and information about the advancement of democracy in countries throughout the world. The institute is affiliated with the American Federation of Teachers.

The American Democracy Project for Civic Engagement
www.nytimes.com/college/collegespecial2/

Created as a collaboration between the American Association of State Colleges and Universities, its member colleges and universities, and the New York Times Knowledge Network, the American Democracy Project for Civic Engagement is a national initiative that seeks to foster informed civic engagement in the United States. The project involves 205 campuses representing more than 1.7 million students.

The Annenberg Classroom
www.annenbergclassroom.org

This site developed for teachers provides teaching and learning materials created by the Annenberg Foundation Trust at Sunnylands that are dedicated to the education of citizens for responsible and effective participation in a constitutional democracy. Teachers can find lesson plans, books, video and audio resources, and classroom handouts on a wide range of issues.

Center for Civic Education
www.civiced.org

The Center for Civic Education in Calabasas, California, is a national and international leader in teaching and learning about constitutional democracy. This site includes various kinds of information and materials for teaching and learning about civic education and democracy.

Constitutional Rights Foundation
www.crf-usa.org

The Constitutional Rights Foundation, located in California, is a leader in education about the U.S. Bill of Rights. This site offers teaching and learning materials about rights and citizenship in the constitutional democracy of the United States.

Freedom House
www.freedomhouse.org

This nongovernmental organization conducts an annual survey of freedom and democracy in the world. This survey rates every nation-state in the world in terms of several criteria by which it measures the extent to which each country is free or unfree and democratic or nondemocratic. The site presents the results of its annual survey and a variety of information about freedom and democracy in the world.

Justice Learning
www.justicelearning.org

This website on issues of law and justice was created with the support of the Annenberg Foundation Trust at Sunnylands. It includes audio from NPR's Justice Talking and news articles from the New York Times Learning Network as well as an interactive U.S. Constitution and historical timelines.

The National Constitution Center
www.constitutioncenter.org

The National Constitution Center is an interactive museum dedicated to increasing public understanding of, and appreciation for, the U.S. Constitution, its history, and its contemporary relevance. Located within Independence National Historical Park in Philadelphia, the center also runs a number of national educational programs promoting democracy and constitutionalism.

National Endowment for Democracy

www.ned.org

The National Endowment for Democracy (NED) is a U.S. government agency that promotes democracy in all regions of the world. It maintains a Democracy Resource Center that disseminates information about democracy. This site includes information about events and issues related to democracy in all parts of the world.

U.S. Agency for International Development (USAID)

www.usaid.gov

The USAID's Center for Democracy and Governance helps countries around the world to create and sustain democratic institutions. This site provides information about democratic development in countries throughout the world.

World Movement for Democracy

www.wmd.org

This is a global network of organizations that promote democracy. The site includes position papers and research about democracy throughout the world.

INDEX

Abrams v. *United States*, 33

Accountability, 7, 16, 18, 43, 44, 65, 78, 82

African Americans. *See* Black Americans

Algeria, 79, 97

Amendments (U.S. Constitution), 18, 34, 37, 40, 50, 74

Angola, 79

Argentina, 41, 76, 78, 90

Aristotle, 98

Articles of Confederation, 39

Associations, voluntary. *See* Civil society

Australia, 41, 71, 97

Authoritarianism, 17

Authority, 17, 74

Belgium, 41

Bill of Rights, 86

Black Americans, 34–35, 49

Branches of government. *See* Executive branch, Judicial branch,
       Legislative branch

Brandeis, Louis D., 93

Brazil, 41, 74, 76, 90

Burma (Myanmar), 79, 96

Canada, 41, 62, 71

Checks and balances, 42, 63–64, 77, 90

China, 14, 74–75, 79, 96

Churchill, Winston, 13

Citizen, 5–6, 18, 19, 36, 82, 98–99

Citizenship, 6, 18, 19, 20–21, 38, 82, 83

Civic education, 20–21

Civic engagement, 19, 65

Civic identity, 18, 34, 82

Civil liberties, 56

Civil society, 22–23, 35, 43, 44, 53

Command economy, 60, 61

Common good, 6, 19, 24–25, 82

Communitarian, 24

Confederations, 39

Congress, U.S., 77–78, 90. *See also* House of Representatives,
       Legislative branch, Senate

Consent of the people, 7, 17, 73, 79
Conservative Party, 70
Conservatives, 55
Constituents, 31
Constitution, 7–8, 18, 19, 26–27, 28–30, 31, 42–43, 46, 73, 88–89
Constitution of the United States, 26, 27, 29, 31, 38, 45, 46, 49, 56, 73–74, 80, 87, 88, 90–91. *See also* Amendments (U.S. Constitution)
Constitutional democracy. *See* Democracy, constitutional
Constitutional limitations, 10
Constitutional monarchy, 62, 79
Constitutional republic, 62
Constitutional review, 47–48, 63
Constitutional supremacy, 88
Constitutionalism, 8, 23, 28–30, 98
Constitutions, unwritten, 27
Cuba, 79, 96
Czech Republic, 52, 56, 58, 74

Declaration of Independence, 37, 52–53, 73, 85–86
Democracy in America, 23, 25, 99
Democracy, ancient Greek, 5–6
Democracy, constitutional, 18, 19, 31–32, 33
Democracy, origins, 5–6
Democracy, representative, 8, 31–32
Democracy, strengths and weaknesses, 11–13
Democracy, unlimited, 32
Democratic Party, 70, 95
Denmark, 79, 94
Direct democracy, 10
Distributive justice, 50–51
Diversity, 18, 33–35, 52
Divine right to rule, 17
Division of powers. *See* Federalism
Dual sovereignty, 40
Due process of law, 28, 37, 50, 84

Economy. *See* Command economy, Market economy
Education. *See* Civic education
Elections, 7, 16, 17, 31, 32, 36, 43, 48, 63, 65, 70–72, 74, 84
Enlightenment, 83, 85
Equality, 18, 37–38, 49, 52, 88–89

Estonia, 16, 52, 66, 71, 72
Ethnic groups, 34, 35, 41
Executive branch, 42, 62, 76–78, 90–91

Fascism, 12, 43
Federal Republic of Germany. *See* Germany
Federalism, 39–41, 43, 97
Federalist, The, 9, 10, 29, 40–41, 45, 47, 49, 76,
  80, 92
France, 52, 97
Freedom of assembly, 22, 23, 33, 34
Freedom of association, 22, 23, 33, 34
Freedom of expression, 33, 44, 84
Freedom of press, 16, 22, 23, 33
Freedom of religion, 33, 84
Freedom of speech, 16, 22, 23, 33

Germany, 14, 35, 41, 43, 62, 97
Government, constitutional, 26–27, 42–43
Government power, limits on, 26, 42–43, 54, 57
Great Britain. *See* United Kingdom
Greece, ancient, 5–6, 83
Guinea, 96

Hamilton, Alexander, 9, 29–30, 45, 47, 76
Hereditary nobility, 80
Hereditary rule, 79, 81
Holmes, Oliver Wendell, Jr., 33
House of Representatives, 77, 90
Human rights, 37, 43, 49, 52–53, 86–87. *See also* Rights

Impeachment, 78
Independent media, 16, 22, 23, 44. *See also* Mass media
India, 34, 41, 94, 97
Individualism, 24
Initiative, 65–67
Interest group, 68
International Covenant on Economic, Social, and Cultural
  Rights, 86–87
International Covenant on Civil and Political Rights, 86–87
Iran, 69, 79–80
Islam, 69

Israel, 27
Italy, 18, 43, 62, 79, 83

Japan, 24, 61, 62, 79
Jay, John, 9
Jefferson, Thomas, 32, 57, 58
Judicial branch, 42, 45, 46, 76, 77, 90, 91
Judicial independence, 45, 91
Judicial review, 46–48, 63, 77, 91
Justice, 49–51, 54, 88–89

King, Martin Luther, Jr., 49

Labor unions, 22
Labour Party, 70
Lander, 35, 97
Latvia, 62
Law, rule of, 16, 23, 26–27, 42, 88–89
Legislative branch, 42–43, 62, 76, 77–78, 90–91
Legitimacy, 17
Liberal democracy, 53
Liberal model of democracy, 67, 95
Liberal republicanism, 83
Liberalism, 52–55, 82, 83
Libertarianism, 54, 55
Liberty, 7, 8–9, 52, 54, 56–57, 95
Libya, 79, 97
Limited government, 28–30, 42–43, 52, 91
Lincoln, Abraham, 13
Lithuania, 16, 37, 63, 66, 74
Local governments, 39–40, 97
Locke, John, 83, 85

Madison, James, 9, 10, 29–30, 32, 40, 49, 57, 80, 92, 99
Majority rule, 6, 31–32, 58–59, 80
Marbury v. *Madison*, 47
Market economy, 35, 43, 53, 60–61
Marshall, John, 47
Mass media, 16, 22, 36, 44. *See also* Independent media
Massachusetts constitution, 27, 46
Mexico, 41, 76
Mill, John Stuart, 83

Minority rights, 6, 31, 32, 58–59, 80
Monarchy, 62, 79
Montesquieu, 83
Multiple-party systems, 36, 70–71, 72
Myers v. *United States*, 93

Natural rights, 85–86
Nazism, 12, 43, 86
Netherlands, 48, 62, 63, 79
New Zealand, 27, 62, 63, 71
No confidence vote, 63
Nondemocratic republics, 79–80, 96
Nongovernmental organizations, 65, 68–69. *See also* Civil society
North Korea, 14, 79, 96
Norway, 62, 79, 94

Ombudsman, 16
Ordered liberty, 8–9, 56–57

Pakistan, 79
Panama, 90
Parliamentary democracies, 71
Parliamentary system, 62–64, 77, 78, 92
Participation, 20, 22, 44, 65–67, 82
Participatory model of democracy, 67, 83
Passport, 18
Philippines, 76, 90
Pluralism, 68–69
Poland, 24
Polis, 5
Political participation, 65–67. *See also* Participation
Political party, 34, 36, 62, 70–72
Popular sovereignty, 7, 73–75, 82
Portugal, 28
President, 63, 90
Presidential system, 63–64, 76–78, 90
Pressure group, 68
Prime minister, 62, 63
Privacy rights, 84
Procedural justice, 50
Property rights, 60, 84
Proportional representation, 71–72
Public good. *See* Common good

Racial segregation laws, 49
Referendum, 65–66, 67
Representative democracy. *See* Democracy, representative
Representatives, 79
Republic, 62, 79–81
Republican Party, 70, 95
Republicanism, 82–83
Responsibilities of citizens, 19, 82
Rights, 6, 84–87
    of citizens, 19, 83
    constitutional, 22–23
    human, 37, 43, 49, 52–53, 86–87
    political, 7, 84, 87
    property, 60, 84
    social and economic, 87, 94–95
Rome, ancient, 83
Rousseau, Jean-Jacques, 83
Rule of law, 23, 28–30, 37–38, 45, 52, 60, 88–89

Saudi Arabia, 69
Senate, 77, 90
Separation of powers, 90–93
Single-representative district system, 71, 72
Slovak Republic, 52, 53
Social democracy, 51, 94–95
Socialism, 54
South Korea, 79
Soviet Union, 14, 22, 43, 44, 61, 69, 79
Spain, 62, 79
State or nation-state, 6, 96
State or provincial governments, 39–40, 97
Sudan, 79, 97
Supremacy clause, 39–40
Supreme Court, U.S., 29, 47, 77, 90
Swaziland, 97
Sweden, 16, 51, 79, 94
Switzerland, 34, 41
Syria, 79, 96

Tocqueville, Alexis de, 14, 23, 25, 99
Totalitarian governments, 22
Two-party systems, 36, 70, 71
Tyranny, protections against, 8, 29, 32, 48, 58

Union of Soviet Socialist Republics (USSR). *See* Soviet Union
Unitary state, 97
Unitary system of government, 39
United Kingdom, 27, 48, 62, 63, 70, 71, 79, 85.
United Nations, 86–87, 96
United States of America
    citizenship, 19
    and common good, 24
    democracy in, 31–32
    diversity in, 34–35
    and elections, 36
    and equality, 37–38
    and federalism, 39–41, 97
    and judicial review, 46–47
    and liberalism, 52–53
    and political parties, 70, 71
    and popular sovereignty, 73–74
    presidential system, 76–78
    referendums and initiatives, 66
    as republic, 80–81
    and rights, 84–86
    separation of powers, 90–93
    and social democracy, 94–95
Universal Declaration of Human Rights, 87
Unwritten constitutions, 27
U.S. Constitution. *See* Constitution of the United States
U.S. Supreme Court. *See* Supreme Court, U.S.
Uzbekistan, 79

Veto power, 62, 90
Vietnam, 96
Virtue, civic, 21, 82, 98–99
Voluntary associations. *See* Civil society

Welfare state liberals, 54–55
Welfare states, 51
World War II, 87

Zimbabwe, 79, 96

THE ANNENBERG FOUNDATION TRUST AT SUNNYLANDS

The Annenberg Foundation Trust at Sunnylands was established in 2001 by the Annenberg Foundation to advance public understanding of and appreciation for democracy and to address serious issues facing the country and the world.

The Trust convenes:

- leaders of the United States to focus on ways to improve the functioning of the three branches of government, the press, and public schools;
- educators to determine how to better teach about the Constitution and the fundamental principles of democracy;
- leaders of major social institutions including learned societies to determine how these institutions can better serve the public and the public good;
- scholars addressing ways to improve the well-being of the nation in such areas as media, education, and philanthropy.

The Annenberg Classroom (*www.annenbergclassroom. org*), *www.justicelearning.org*, and a collection of books on the U.S. Constitution, democracy, and related topics, are all projects of the Annenberg Foundation Trust at Sunnylands.

John J. Patrick is a professor emeritus of education at Indiana University, Bloomington. From 1986 to 2004, he was also director of Indiana University's Social Studies Development Center. Patrick is the author or co-author of more than one hundred publications—including books, chapters in books, and articles in journals—on topics in civic education, history education, U.S. history, and political science or government. His books include: *The Supreme Court of the United States: A Student Companion, The Bill of Rights: A History in Documents, Founding the Republic: A Documentary History,* and *How to Teach the Bill of Rights.* He is the co-author of *The Oxford Guide to United States Government, American Political Behavior, Civics Today,* and *Constitutional Debates on Freedom of Religion.*

Patrick was a member of the framework development committees and planning committees for the National Assessment of Educational Progress (NAEP) in Civics and the NAEP in U.S. History. He has been a consultant, lecturer, and seminar director in professional development programs for teachers of history, civics, and government throughout the United States. He has also been a consultant to several state departments of education in the United States and to many curriculum centers and organizations pertaining to civic education.

Since 1991, he has directed or participated in democracy education projects and programs in several post-communist countries, such as Bosnia-Herzegovina, Czech Republic, Estonia, Latvia, Lithuania, and Poland. He has also participated in democracy education programs in several Latin American countries, most recently in Argentina. In 2002, in recognition of his international democracy education work, Patrick received Indiana University's John W. Ryan Award for distinguished contributions to international programs. In 2003, the governor of Indiana gave him the Sagamore of the Wabash Award for his outstanding contributions to civic education. In 2005, he was the first recipient of the Indiana State Bar Association's Civic Education Award.